Loveology

We want to hear from you. Please send your comments about this book to us in care of zreview@zondervan.com. Thank you.

ZONDERVAN

Loveology
Copyright © 2013 by John Mark Comer

This title is also available as a Zondervan ebook. Visit www.zondervan.com/ebooks.

Requests for information should be addressed to:

Zondervan, *Grand Rapids, Michigan 49530*

Library of Congress Cataloging-in-Publication Data
  Comer, John Mark, 1980–
    Loveology : God, love, sex, marriage, and the never-ending story of male and female / John
  Mark Comer. — First [edition].
        pages cm
    ISBN 978-0-310-33726-3 (hardcover)
        1. Man-woman relationships — Religious aspects — Christianity. 2. Marriage — Religious
    aspects — Christianity. I. Title.
    BT705.8.C66   2014
    261.8'35 — dc23   2013032615

Cover design: Ryan Wesley Peterson
Interior design: Ryan Wesley Peterson

Printed in the United States of America

14 15 16 17 18 19 /DCI/ 22 21 20 19 18 17 16 15 14 13 12 11 10 9 8 7 6 5 4 3 2 1

Loveology

God. Love. Marriage. Sex.

And the never-ending story of male and female.

John Mark Comer

With refreshing honesty, wit, and compassion, John Mark Comer delivers a compelling dare to claim (or reclaim) purpose and freedom on the lifelong journey of love, marriage, and sex. Authored in the tension of biblical depth and personal vulnerability, *Loveology* offers clarity and hope to a generation in desperate need of it. I recommend this book to anyone seeking truth and direction as they navigate the murky waters of postmodern relationships and sexuality.

Todd Proctor, lead pastor of Rock Harbor Church, Costa Mesa, California

In a time when people are drowning in a sea of definitions, my friend John Mark Comer has brilliantly defined love, marriage, and sexuality in ways that find rescue in the ways of the kingdom and teachings of Jesus. This is a much-needed tool in a culture where so many lack clarity.

Chuck Bomar, pastor of Colossae Church and author of *Better Off without Jesus*

John Mark Comer is a friend of mine who doesn't just talk about love; he's been living it. This is the kind of book you'll want to pick up to read, but then you'll want to put it down and go do things. Big things. Things that point you and others toward a big God who has in mind big love for the world.

Bob Goff, author of *Love Does* and honorary consul for the Republic of Uganda

My concept of sexuality has been greatly renewed through John Mark's thorough explanation of God's heart for it. I cannot begin to express the impeccable timing of *Loveology* for my generation.

Michael, 25

Finally. Someone who will talk about love, marriage, and sexuality in a way that doesn't sound like a textbook or an awkward conversation with your parents or a "just say no" campaign. *Loveology* wakes up a conversation I didn't know I needed to have, and it will leave a lasting impression for years to come.

Allison Vesterfelt, author of *Packing Light*

I greatly respect John Mark Comer. He is a close friend and solid teacher. He clearly understands the obstacles facing this generation and powerfully speaks into the pain and frustration so many people are facing. Everyone would benefit from the truth laid out so plainly in *Loveology.*

Kevin Palau, president of the Luis Palau Association

It is so refreshing to have a real and honest study about love, sexuality, and relationships for what they are. Gifts from the Lord.

Tim, 25

John Mark has written a great book on the theology of love that is right in all the right ways. Right tone, right truth, right timing. We need this book to navigate the confusing waters of modern sexuality. I highly recommend this read.

Dave Lomas, lead pastor of Reality San Francisco

Loveology is a compassionate and courageous manifesto for the most sexually confused generation in human history. With grace and truth, John Mark shows how the revolutionary good news of Jesus intersects with our sexuality and relationships. Highly recommended.

Mike Erre, senior pastor of First Evangelical Free Church, Fullerton, California, and author of *The Jesus of Suburbia*

John Mark's lifelong propensity to question everything has led him to flip upside down the current Christian cultural thinking about dating and marriage. My brother has shaped the way I approach love.

John Mark's little brother, Matthew, 21

In a culture where marriage is optional and sex is cheap, people need to know how to navigate the deep issues of love, marriage, and sex, all while following Jesus. *Loveology* is a great resource to do just that.

Rick McKinley, lead pastor of Imago Dei Community, Portland, Oregon, and author of *This Beautiful Mess*

My husband and I heard "loveology" at the beginning of our relationship, and it changed our entire view on love and dating. It exposed and shattered all the "Hollywood movie" lies that were embedded in our minds and replaced them with God's original design. Following the *Loveology* principles gave our relationship a sense of direction, saved us from making a lot of painful mistakes many couples make, and answered a ton of questions.

Naomi and Isaiah, 22 and 24, married for seven months

Love is at the forefront of the experience of what it means to be human. We can choose to try to figure it out on our own, or we can choose to see how the designer of love intended us to experience all this. *Loveology* guides us straight into the heart of God, who created this wondrous, powerful experience of love, romance, sex, marriage, masculinity, and femininity.

Dan Kimball, teaching pastor at Vintage Faith Church, Santa Cruz, California

John Mark's *Loveology* material provided my wife and me a generationally relevant framework from which to discuss (during our long-distance relationship) the complex topics of romance, dating, sex, and family. His teachings unashamedly address the awkward and messy world of romance in a biblical and countercultural way. Read this book if you are single, dating, engaged, or married. And then read it again.

Benjamin, 22

John Mark Comer offers a fresh, biblical perspective on love, relationships, and sexuality in a world that has almost forgotten what these words really mean. A great read on God's original intent and how it should look in our lives today.

Phil Wickham, singer/songwriter and worship leader

Loveology brings clarity to the "why" behind our questions about love, sex and marriage. (You know, those topics we rarely talk about …) Instead of giving a formula, John Mark Comer relays what he has learned from extensive study and transforms it into clear and humble teachings that will bring us to our own illumination moments and to a deeper understanding of God's love for us.

Joy Eggerichs, director of Love and Respect NOW

Loveology challenges our thinking about the purpose and plan for sex in marriage and provides insight into what Scripture actually says about it. John Mark married us, and we have front-row seats as a part of his community to see him work this out in his own marriage. Read this book and start putting into practice the things you learn here.

Matt and Anna, John Mark's newly married neighbors

The path

Genesis 2v15–25

The LORD God took the man and put him in the Garden of Eden to work it and take care of it. And the LORD God commanded the man, "You are free to eat from any tree in the garden; but you must not eat from the tree of the knowledge of good and evil, for when you eat from it you will certainly die." The LORD God said, "It is not good for the man to be alone. I will make a helper suitable for him." Now the LORD God had formed out of the ground all the wild animals and all the birds in the sky. He brought them to the man to see what he would name them; and whatever the man called each living creature, that was its name. So the man gave names to all the livestock, the birds in the sky and all the wild animals. But for Adam no suitable helper was found. So the LORD God caused the man to fall into a deep sleep; and while he was sleeping, he took one of the man's ribs and then closed up the place with flesh. Then the LORD God made a woman from the rib he had taken out of the man, and he brought her to the man. The man said, "This is now bone of my bones and flesh of my flesh; she shall be called 'woman,' for she was taken out of man." That is why a man leaves his father and mother and is united to his wife, and they become one flesh. Adam and his wife were both naked, and they felt no shame.

The beginning

In the beginning God created Adam.

Then he made Eve.

And ever since we've been picking up the pieces.

Love and hate.

Marriage and divorce.

Sexuality and adultery.

Romance and heartache.

Everything we know (and think we know) about love. First dates, men down on one knee, the Hallmark cards with elderly couples who look exactly the same—it all started with two naked humans in a garden.

This book is about what's right in male-female relationships—what God created and called "good" all those years ago. And this book is about what's wrong—about fallout east of Eden.

We are the sons of Adam and the daughters of Eve. We were

created "male and female." We were set up to love. To absorb the love of God into our bloodstream and then to share it with another human being.

But we don't live in a garden anymore. We're the exact opposite of "naked and unashamed." We wear clothes — some of us more than others, a-hem! — and far too often, our clothes are a cheap facade to mask our guilt and shame.

When it comes to love, we are both the victim and the perpetrator of the crime. Because we are human, we love, but because we love, we *bleed*. Love is the source of our highest highs and lowest lows. Love is joy and laughter and gift and freedom and faith and healing, but when love goes south, it's a knife to the chest.

If you're a child of divorce, you feel the tension. You know better than anybody what happens when love breaks down, yet you are drawn to love like a moth to a flame. It's in your blood. Children grow up dreaming of marriage. Little boys want to marry their moms. Little girls put on white dresses and play "march down the aisle." You're no different. But at the same time you live under a dark cloud of paranoia. Will you make the exact same mistake as your parents? Will you become another statistic? Will your dream become a nightmare?

And there's good reason. The odds are not in your favor.

Fifty percent of marriages end in divorce.[1]

Did you catch that? *Fifty percent.*

Because we hear that stat all the time, we grow numb to how gut-wrenching and nauseating it is. The chances of your marriage lasting more than a few short years are fifty-fifty.

Toss a coin into the air. Call heads or tails. Slap it on your wrist.

Those are the odds.

What happened? How did we get from the Garden of Eden to *this*? And how can we get back on track?

Ervat davar

The writer Matthew tells a story about Jesus fielding questions on divorce. Divorce was rampant in Jesus' day, just as it is in ours. Marriage was unraveling at the seams. And one day the Pharisees showed up at Jesus' door asking for his take …

"Is it lawful for a man to divorce his wife for any and every reason?"[2]

In today's language, "Is God ever okay with divorce? If so, when?"

A quick bit of history to make sense of the Pharisees' question. In the first century, there was a raging debate over an obscure text in the Torah (the first five books of the Bible). In *Deuteronomy*, Moses said, "If a man marries a woman who becomes displeasing to him because he finds something indecent about her, and he writes her a certificate of divorce ..."[3]

The phrase "something indecent" is *ervat davar* in Hebrew, and it's just as ambiguous in the original language as it sounds in English. What did Moses mean by "something indecent"? There were two sides in the debate.

On one side was the school of Shammai, which followed the teachings of the right-wing, conservative rabbi named Shammai. He said there was one, *and only one*, reason a man could divorce his wife — adultery. That act broke the bond of marriage with the hammer of infidelity. That was his interpretation of "something indecent." Sadly, Shammai's interpretation was the minority view.

On the other side was the school of Hillel, the leftist progressive of the day. Rabbi Hillel said a man could divorce his wife for "any and every reason." If she gains five pounds, that sounds like "something indecent" — divorce her. If "you aren't happy anymore" — divorce her. As crazy as it sounds, we have records of Hillel's teachings where he says things like, "If she burns the toast — *ervat davar*! Divorce her!"[4] For obvious reasons, Hillel's take was by far the popular, majority view.

And to clarify, Hillel's interpretation was called the "any and every reason" clause and was written on marriage certificates around the time of Jesus.

Now back to the Pharisees' question ...

"Is it lawful for a man to divorce his wife for *any and every reason*?"

The Pharisees are essentially asking Jesus, "Where do you stand on divorce? With Hillel? Or with Shammai? What's your take?"

Jesus' answer speaks volumes ...

"'Haven't you read,' he replied, 'that at the beginning the Creator "made them male and female," and said, "For this reason a man will leave his father and mother and be united to his wife, and the two will become one flesh"? So they are no longer two, but one. Therefore what God has joined together, let no one separate.'"

In other words, "You're asking the wrong question."

The question you should be asking is, "What is God's *dream* for marriage?" And to answer *that* question, Jesus takes the Pharisees back to the beginning. He quotes from one of the first stories in the Scriptures. And it turns out to be a love story ...

Bone of my bones

In the Genesis narrative, God looks down on the world and sees that Adam is a lonely human on a solitary planet. "It is not good for the man to be alone," he says.[5]

So God does something about it. He causes a deep sleep to fall over Adam. Then he takes a rib from the man's side, and from that rib — from Adam's *bones* — he creates Eve.

Adam wakes up to a dream. And he *sings* over the woman ...

> "This is now bone of my bones
>   and flesh of my flesh;
> she shall be called 'woman,'
>   for she was taken out of man."

Notice that the first words out of a human's mouth in the Scriptures are a love song.

And with a smile on his face, God joins in the song and says, "That is why a man leaves his father and mother and is united to his wife, and they become one flesh."

When God said that, God created marriage.

Did you catch that?

God created marriage.

This whole thing was his idea. Love, marriage, sexuality, romance — it all began in the mind of God. It was his imagination, his creative genius, that thought it all up.

Marriage did not evolve fifty thousand years ago in ancient Mesopotamia as a way to deal with civic litigation. It was embedded into human DNA right from the start.

That's why people from *every culture on the planet* get married. From

Papua New Guinea to New York City, one strand runs through the tapestry of the more than seven billion people on earth—marriage.

Marriage is the product of creation, not culture. Humans get credit for a lot of stuff in the Genesis story. We came up with science and technology and the arts and architecture and urban planning—but not marriage. It goes all the way back to God.

This means that God knows how it's supposed to function. How it's supposed to work. The God who *created* marriage knows what it's supposed to look like.

But somewhere along the way we lost sight of what God intended. We need to circle back to the beginning, to the story that started it all. The reality is that the garden story holds out two truths.

The first is that *love is beautiful.* All those years ago, God created something stunning. Despite the pain, the heartbreak, and the long odds, we keep coming back to the love song that is male and female. Somehow we know, deep in our bones, that it's well worth the risk.

At the same time, though, we all know that *something is wrong.* The beauty of the original creation is still there, but it's been marred and warped.

Something happened in that garden. The serpent found his way into Eden. He came upon Adam and Eve in the beauty of unpolluted, innocent love. Seething with hatred and jealousy, all he could think to do was destroy the first marriage.

God is the creator of life. The serpent is not his equal, *but he is his opposite*. Jesus called him "a murderer from the beginning" and exposed his agenda as one who "comes only to steal and kill and destroy."[6] What God builds up, the serpent tries to tear down. What God sets free, he tries to imprison. What God creates, he tries to deface.

Adam and Eve's love was far too beautiful for the serpent to leave unmolested. All it took was a lie.

God had told them not to eat from "the tree of the knowledge of good and evil," because "when you eat from it you will certainly die." But the serpent whispered in Eve's ear, "You will not certainly die. For God knows that when you eat from it your eyes will be opened, and you will be like God, knowing good and evil."[7]

What was the lie?

That God isn't our lover. That he's not after our joy. That we can't trust him. That God's way isn't the best way. That we know better than God.

And the first humans — gullible and naive — bought the lie.

From there the love story turned into a tragedy. The first place sin wreaked havoc was in Adam and Eve's relationship. Adam blamed his wife. Eve blamed the serpent. Two people at each other's throats — and the first sitcom marriage was born.

It's easy to think of Adam and Eve as stupid. Premodern cavemen one step removed from the apes. But are we any different? Any better?

The reality is that we all face the *exact same choice*. Which tree will we eat from?

Will we buy the lie? Go our own way, thinking we know better than God? Flip a coin and hope for the best? Or will we listen, not to the voice of the serpent, but to the Creator. Will we believe that God's way is the best way? He is the Creator, *and he's good.*

Somewhere along the way we lost the plotline. And if we want to find our way back to Eden, back to "naked and unashamed," then we have to follow the voice of Jesus.

I'll admit it seems a bit strange to take advice on love from a single guy. I guess the life of a wandering rabbi/prophet/Messiah wasn't exactly conducive for romance. Yet we believe that Jesus is the living God come among us.

The God who said, "It is not good for the man to be alone" and the Rabbi who said, "Have you not read …?" are one and the same.

And from the lips of Jesus we get loveology …

Part 1
Love

Ahava

I believe in love at first sight. Well, kind of.

It was the sixteenth of September, 1998. I was at a party with friends, outdoors on a hot summer evening. In the Northwest we get an Indian summer, and September is my favorite time of the year. It was a perfect day—high 70s, but with a soft breeze. The trees over my head were making that swishing sound they do when they flirt with the wind.

In the middle of a conversation, I saw her out of the corner of my eye. She was a vision of long, curly black hair and deep, almond-shaped eyes, and she was walking toward *me*.

You know those guys who are suave with the ladies?

I am not one of them.

Girls make me nervous. I'm clumsy and awkward *on a good day*. And *this* girl—well, let's just say all my fine motor skills went out the window.

I'm sure I was staring. Heck, I was probably drooling. I dropped a pen I'd been fiddling with. "Shoot. I'm such a klutz." Before I could reach down, she walked over and picked it up off the ground. "Here ya go," she said—and all I could do was stare at two of the brown-est eyes I'd ever seen.

She might as well have said, "Will you marry me?"

I was hooked. There was something about her smile. It was warm and disarming. She was calm. Relaxed. Soothing. Everything I'm not.

And she was *beautiful*. I mean, crazy, over-the-top, don't-even-try-or-you-will-make-a-fool-of-yourself beautiful.

Everything after the pen is hazy. I'm sure I muddled through a short dialogue and embarrassed myself. But I remember I didn't sleep that night.

Or the next.

Or the next.

She took over my mind. Her troops marched in and colonized my imagination. All I could think about was seeing her again.

A few weeks later I said to a friend, "I think she's it."

He was annoyed, understandably. "What? You barely know her!"

And he was right. It was an impetuous thing to say. I barely knew her. But that didn't matter for one simple reason: I was *in love*.

I had no clue what was coming around the bend. No idea that our picture-perfect romance would be followed by a less-than-ideal marriage. That my entire paradigm for our relationship was seriously off-kilter. That hard stuff was brewing on the horizon.

But I'm getting ahead of myself.

At this point in my story, I was awash in feelings of romantic love—attraction, tension, mystery, allure. I was in love, deeper than I'd ever been. Drowning, and loving every minute of it.

Time for a definition

In love. What does that even mean?

"Love" is a junk drawer we dump all sorts of ideas into, just because we don't have anywhere else to put them.

I "love" God, and I "love" fish tacos. See the problem?

The way we use the word is so broad, so generic, that I'm not sure we understand it anymore. How should we define *love*?

To some, love is tolerance. I hear this all the time in my city. The idea is that rather than judge people, we should "love" them. And what people mean is that we shouldn't call out something as wrong. After all, as long as it's not hurting anybody, who are we to judge? And while this sounds nice, and forward, and progressive, it doesn't work for me. The opposite of love isn't hate. It's apathy. And there's a fine line between tolerance and apathy.

To many of us, love is passion for a *thing*. It's the word we call on to conjure up all our feelings of affection. We *love* hiking, or we *love* that new record by the band you've never heard of, or we *love* chips and guac.

When we aim the word at *people*, we usually mean the exact same thing. When we say we love someone, we mean we have *deep feelings of affection* because they make us feel alive all over again—adventurous, brave, happy.

Love, by this definition, is pure, unfiltered emotion. And your role in love is *passive*. It's something that happens to you. Think of the phrase "fall in love." It's like tripping over a rock or a curb. And it's fantastic. But there's a dark underbelly to feeling this kind of romantic love. If we can fall into it, then we can fall *out* of it.

What happens when the emotions fade or disappear? What happens when someone *else* makes you feel even *more* alive? Then you have a serious problem on your hands.

If you're dating, it's not the end of the world. You break up and move on.

But what if you're engaged? Married? Do you stay together, even though you're not "in love" anymore? Or do you go the way of the 50 percent?

I believe that marriage is for life. Remember what Jesus said? "What God has joined together, *let no one separate.*" I stand with Jesus, which is why I think we need a redefinition of love that will stand up to the frontal assault of life. And we find that redefinition in the Scriptures.

There's a letter in the New Testament called *1 John.* It was written by a guy named — well, I'm sure you figured that part out. John was one of Jesus' disciples. He spent three years with Love-incarnate, and he was known as "the disciple whom Jesus loved."[1] That pretty much makes him an expert on the subject.

John's definition of love is blatant and clear-cut — "This is love: not that we loved God, but that he loved us and sent his Son as an atoning sacrifice for our sins."[2]

Love = Jesus on the cross.

There you have it, in black-and-white.

If you want to know what love looks like, don't look at a dictionary. Look at a Jewish prophet crucified outside Jerusalem. Look at God in the flesh, giving his life away for the world.

Does that sound anything like "deep feelings of affection"?

Don't get me wrong. I have no doubt that Jesus was *feeling* something in that moment. It was "for the joy set before him" that "he endured the cross."[3] Love *is* emotion, but it's gotta be more than that.

Notice that John uses the word *love* as both a noun and a verb. "This is *love* ... that he *loved* us ..."

Love is a noun *and* a verb.

Put another way, love is a feeling *and* an action.

When it comes to the feeling of love, you're in the passenger seat. As I said before, your role is passive. It's something that happens to you. But with the action of love, you're at the wheel. Your role is active. It's something you do.

And the feeling of love isn't bad. There's nothing wrong with romantic feelings. The first song (Adam's poem in Genesis 2), and the longest song (*Song of Songs*) are both celebrations of romantic love. If you are "in love" — enjoy it. We are emotional creatures. God made us that way. Romantic feelings are a gift from the Creator God.

But at its root, feelings can be selfish. Behind all the flowers and poetry and twitterpation, there's a narcissist hiding in the closet.

When we say "I love you," what we often mean is, "When I'm around you, I feel happy. You make me feel better about myself. Comfortable in my own skin." Now, that's not all bad, but you don't have to be a psychologist to figure out where that road leads.

Love, the action, the *verb*, is a whole other story. At its core, love — as defined by Jesus on the cross — is *self-giving*.

Over and over again, the authors of the New Testament point to Jesus' death on the cross as the ultimate act of self-giving love.

In another place, John writes, "For God so loved the world that he *gave* his one and only Son ..."[4]

The prolific author Paul writes that God "did not spare his own Son, but *gave* him up for us all ..."[5]

And in Paul's mind, Jesus' death is the model for how a man is to love a woman. Later he writes, "Husbands, love your wives, just as Christ loved the church and *gave* himself up for her ..."[6] Husband or wife, male or female, we can *all* take a lesson from that.

Why love is about washing feet

This idea of Jesus as the model for how we are to love each other sounds docile and tame and cliché, but when we actually read about the life of Jesus, it's stunning.

I love the story in *The Gospel of John* where Jesus washes the disciples' feet.[7] In the first century, foot washing was the job of a servant or, worse, a slave. The streets were unpaved. Filled with dirt and muck and animal droppings. People walked around in sandals, not shoes, and by the end of the day, their feet were ... well, use your imagination. But Jesus, *the embodiment of the creator God,* the God who made humans from the dust on the street right outside the door, picks up a towel and starts to clean the grime from between John's toes.

Imagine the mayor of a city pulling up a manhole cover, dropping down into the sewer, and starting to shovel crap. Now dial that up by a factor of a gillion, and you're starting to see what's going on in the story.

When Jesus finished with the disciples' feet, he asked, "Do you understand what I have done for you?" Almost as if to point out the staggering implications of what just happened. "You call me 'Teacher' and 'Lord,' and rightly so, for that is what I am. Now that I, your Lord and Teacher, have washed your feet, you also should wash one another's feet. I have set you an example that you should do as I have done for you."[8]

Jesus' life is *the* example for how to love.

It's that easy.

And that difficult.

Because to Jesus, love is serving. It's cleaning garbage off his feet. It's wiping grime from between her toes. It's choosing — *choosing* of your own free will — to play the role of the servant, the least important person in the room.

And that is not easy to do.

That's why love is commanded by God in the Scriptures. Jesus said, "A new *command* I give you: *Love* one another." [9] In fact, Jesus said the greatest command in all of the Torah (the Bible of his day) was to "love the Lord your God … love your neighbor as yourself." [10]

Remember how we talked about the difference between the feeling of love and the action of love? You cannot command feelings. You can only command actions. God does not command you to *like* your neighbor or to have *deep feelings of affection* for your neighbor. He commands you to *love* your neighbor.

But what kind of love?

The Jesus kind of love. Cross-shaped love. The down-on-your-knees-with-a-smelly-towel-in-your-hands sort of love.

When you strip love down to its essence — its core — it's *self-giving*. Yes, it's romantic feelings, but we have to understand that it's so much more.

Ahava

In Hebrew, there's this word *ahava*, and it's a godsend as we learn about love. In English, we have just the one word — *love* — to denote a wide range of positive emotion, but in Hebrew, there's a handful, and each one draws out a specific nuance.

You can *rayah* somebody. That's the love you feel for a friend. In fact, it can be translated "friend" or "companion." In one ancient

Hebrew story, a man says to his girlfriend, "Arise, my *rayah*, my beautiful one, come with me."[11] *Rayah* is when you want to get out of town, spend time together, talk, play, goof off, and just do life shoulder to shoulder. We all need a good *rayah*.

Then there's *dod*. This word is used in the opening line of *Song of Songs*. The woman says, "Let him kiss me with the kisses of his mouth — for your *dod* is more delightful than wine."[12] *Dod* is when you see a woman and you instantly want to make babies with her, when you see a guy and all you can think about is what his skin would feel like up against yours. *Dod* is when keeping your hands in your pockets takes every ounce of strength in your being.

We'll get to *dod* later ...

For now, let's drill down on this word *ahava*. This kind of love is something more. Something deeper, wider, and stronger. It's both of the above — *rayah* and *dod* — plus some. It's a love that goes down to the soul, the deepest part of your being. It's a love that is unbending and unflinching, and that doesn't take no for an answer. It's relentless and implacable.

At the climax of the poem called *Song of Songs*, there's a moving stanza ...

> Place me like a seal over your heart,
>   like a seal on your arm;
> for *ahava* is as strong as death,
>   its jealousy unyielding as the grave.

It burns like blazing fire,
    like a mighty flame.
Many waters cannot quench *ahava*;
    rivers cannot sweep it away.[13]

Are you picking up on the imagery?

Ahava is like death, like the grave—an unstoppable force that we are powerless to fight off.

Ahava is like a fire out of control, engulfing forests and cities. It cannot be quenched.

And *ahava* is like a tsunami, a tidal wave of fierce, unbridled power bearing down on the world.

The point of the poetry is that *ahava* is strong. Feelings, no matter how vivid, in the long run, are weak. They come and go. But *ahava* has resolve. Staying power. It has that word we all tend to avoid— *commitment*. Over time, it builds up a head of steam, and it breaks through every obstacle. It's a love of the heart, and a love of the will.

My grandparents on my mother's side have been married for sixty years this summer, but a few months ago the doctor found a tumor on my grandma's brain. They rushed her into surgery, and right now she's in recovery. She can barely string together a sentence, but my grandfather is right at her side, 24/7. And here's the crazy part— they are more "in love" than ever before. That's *ahava*.

Ahava is the one and only kind of love that will carry a relationship past the early "deep feelings of affection" and through the whole of life — decades of highs and lows, marriage and family, a career and unemployment, suffering and celebration, sickness and health, and well into the epilogue of life.

You can't build a marriage on deep feelings of affection alone, because they're unreliable. *Flaky* would be an understatement. And you can't build a relationship just on *rayah*. Friendship is vital, but you need an extra spark, something more. *Dod* isn't enough either. No matter how beautiful he or she is, over time, the body will start to wrinkle and age and decay. What happens then? When you still have *decades* of life ahead of you? You need something more.

You need *ahava*.

The Via Dolorosa

I still think about that night so many Septembers ago when I first saw my wife. We were *kids*. I was a freshman in college, eighteen years old. I had no clue what I was getting into. Nobody told me the "deep feelings of affection" fade after a few years. I guess I wasn't listening when the experts said that people who marry young have higher divorce rates.

But even if I had known all that, it wouldn't have changed a thing. I still would have chased her to the world's end. It was feelings that started it all, but we needed something more to make our marriage stick.

Here we are today, with over a decade of marriage under our belts. Three kids, a mortgage, and—thank God—*no* minivan.

And we still love each other.

There are days when we're "in love"—when we *feel* love. When we feel the déjà vu of that first night in the park. And then there are days when we are tired, annoyed, and grouchy, and we feel—let's just say—"other" kinds of emotions for one another.

Through all of life, though, we are *learning* to love each other in Jesus' way. Learning the genius of cross-shaped love.

A while back, I spent a month in Jerusalem. I wanted to learn more about the context for Jesus' life, and there's no better place to do that than in the City of Peace. But a month is a long time to be away from home, and the entire time my mind was turned to my wife. Absence was doing its thing, and I was realizing—all over again—what a gift Tammy is to my life. After endless hours together, I still missed her. I still craved her next to me when I nodded off to sleep.

One night I walked the Via Dolorosa—the road Jesus walked to the cross.[14] It's a moving experience to imagine Jesus—*the creator of everything*—covered in blood and open wounds, tripping his way up the hill to Golgotha. And that evening, walking in the Judean heat, the gravity of Jesus' love hit me all over again. *That's* what Jesus means by "love one another." It's a love that feels—deep, raw, and true emotions. And it's a love that *does*.[15] A love that walks through the crowd of haunting spectators and up to a Roman guard waiting with a hammer and a bag of nails.

Tammy and I have a long way to go, but we're learning about this kind of love. And it's hard, for sure, but it's not all blood, sweat, and tears. The cross is just the beginning of the story. Three days later, the world was rocked by the empty tomb. And resurrection is a beautiful thing. But to get to Easter, Jesus had to go through Good Friday.

The same is true with love. To get to the deep feelings of affection—the romantic love we grow up dreaming about—we have to march down the Via Dolorosa. We have to go the way of the cross.

And the beauty is—we're not the first lover to go down that road.

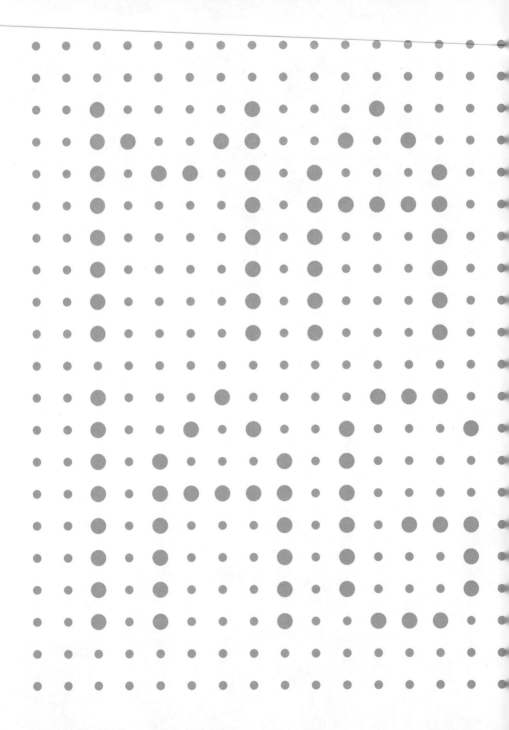

Part 2
Marriage

What's it *for*?

Every good story has a low point. When was the last time you saw a movie, and nothing bad happened in it? A story with no low point is boring. This is Writing 101. We learn in grade school that every good story has a protagonist and an antagonist. It has *conflict.*

Mine is no different.

At first, when my hand brushed up against my wife's, a light tingling feeling shot up my arm.

Early on, when she would walk into the room, my pulse would speed up. I could feel the blood throbbing through my wrists. I was in college at the time, and staying focused in class was murder. My head was dizzy all the time.

But a few years into our marriage, the electric feelings started to fade. My nervous system lost its hypersensitivity. My heart valve readjusted. The vertigo went away.

It didn't take long to figure out that we were different people. *Very* different people. I'm introverted, type A, driven, and high-strung. She's über-social, laid-back, phlegmatic, and go with the flow. We started driving each other *crazy.*

One day we were out running errands. The radio in my car was playing in the background, and between songs there was an advertisement for an online dating service. The spokesman-doctor-expert guy was doing his spiel on how to find the right match in marriage, and his punch line was "opposites attract, and then *attack*."

I reached over and turned off the radio.

Awkward.

Not long after, I started having second thoughts. I was defining love as "deep feelings of affection," and my "love" was fading. And that scared me to death. I'm an idealist. "Good enough" doesn't cut it for me. I want my life to be spectacular. But my marriage was fast becoming ordinary. I wasn't okay with that.

Questions started haunting my thoughts …

Did we make a mistake?

We were so young. Did we jump the gun?

Are we really right for each other?

Why don't I feel the way I used to?

What's wrong with me?

I was sailing without a rudder, blown off course by my doubts and capsized by my fears.

In hindsight, my crisis of faith was based on a faulty understanding of marriage. It wasn't that my marriage was in trouble. It was more like my unrealistic expectations were in trouble. Ninety percent of the problem was in my head.

In short, *I had no idea what marriage was for.*

And I was not alone.

I would argue that far too many of us have a decent idea what marriage is but are confused at best, if not clueless, as to what marriage is for.

Think of the volcanic backlash in the United States over the last few years to the ongoing redefinition of marriage. Millions of Americans are adamant that marriage is *one man, one woman, for life.* Protests and sandwich board signs and slogans and laws and courts and campaigns—a shrinking yet sizable chunk of Americans will not yield to a retelling of the marriage story. And while I think many have gone about it in ways that have been toxic, ignorant, hurtful, and hypocritical, I have to admit that I think this ancient vision is right. All through the Scriptures, God's vision for marriage is a man and a woman, locked together for life.

And as I watch this "war," with both sides angry as hell, I feel the debate is missing something. Despite all the op-eds and sound bites and talking heads, little or nothing is said about what marriage is *for.*

Or put another way, what's the point of marriage?

In a world where half of marriages implode, why get married at all? I think that's a legitimate question. And to answer that question, we have to circle back to the beginning.

The story before the story

The story of the Bible begins and ends with a wedding. In *Genesis* we read about the first wedding of all time — Adam and Eve. And *Revelation* ends with the wedding of heaven and earth.[1]

In fact, God officiates the first wedding. He speaks over Adam and Eve and says, "*That is why* a man leaves his father and mother and is united to his wife, and they become one flesh."[2]

Maybe you're thinking, "Wait, pause, what is why? What is 'why a man leaves his father and mother'?"

To answer *that* question, we have to rewind to the story before the story.

Genesis 1 tells the story of creation from thirty thousand feet. God speaks, and worlds are born. God shapes the land and the sea. He fills the sky with birds. He floods the sea with fish. He populates the land with living creatures. And at the apex, the climactic moment in the narrative, he creates human to take care of his virgin world.

And then Genesis 2 zooms in on a garden called Eden and the first human called Adam — "The LORD God formed a man [*adam* in Hebrew] from the dust of the ground and breathed into his nostrils the breath of life, and the man became a living being. Now the LORD God had planted a garden in the east, in Eden; and there he put the man he had formed ... The LORD God took the man and put him in the Garden of Eden to work it and take care of it."[3]

Eden in Hebrew means "delight." And the story opens with Adam, the protohuman, alone with God in the Garden of Delight. Can you imagine a better life? So far the story's off to a great start, right?

Think again. The very next line is tragic. The story strikes a dissonant, minor chord.

"The LORD God said, 'It is not good for the man to be alone. I will make a helper suitable for him.'"[4]

This comes as a surprise when you read Genesis 1. The narrative is written in semi-poetic language, and the refrain all throughout the story is "God saw that it was good."

God created the land and the sea, and "God saw that it was good." God created plants and trees and vegetation, and "God saw that it was good." God created the sun and moon and stars, and "God saw that it was good."

But right after God created Adam, he said, "It is *not good* for Adam to be alone."

The Hebrew can be translated ... *woops*.

Why is it not good? Well, there are two problems. First, Adam is alone. That's a problem because he's created in the image of God, and God exists in a web of relationships. We'll talk more about this in a bit. For now, just note that Adam was hard-wired for relationships. His aloneness is not a good thing.

The second problem is one of logistics. Adam is called to take care of the garden, but when you do the math, you figure out the garden was the size of a continent.[5] It's not a "garden" in the sense of a park. It's more like a national forest. Millions of square miles of wilderness. Wild. Untamed. And teeming with potentiality.

It's way too much work for one man. He needs help. There's a calling on Adam's life, *but he cannot do it alone*.

Make sure you get that.

And as a result of those two problems, God created woman as "a helper suitable for him." Don't get hung up on the word *helper*. We'll deal with that in the next chapter. Just make sure you get that *he needs help*. So God gets involved.

"He brought her to the man." I love it. *God* brought Eve to Adam. And the Don Juan that he was, Adam started speaking poetry ...

"This is now bone of my bones
    and flesh of my flesh."

And then, after all that, God said, "That is why a man leaves his father ..."

The closing line is an interpolation in the original language. It's almost like God's voice cuts into the story. It's the Creator's way of saying, "Listen up. Pay attention. *This* marriage is a paradigm for *all* marriages." It's not a one-off. It's a template for all marriages to follow. Think about it. Adam didn't have a father or mother to leave. And Eve didn't have any other options. But the story is written in such a way as to make the reader slow down and take notice. This story is ground zero for a theology of marriage. God is saying something we need to get.

Wrapping our heads around what God is saying, however, is going to take an entire chapter ...

Cuatro

Okay, this is the good part. I'm telling you, this rewired the way I think about my marriage from the ground up. In the Genesis story, I see four reasons that God created marriage. And each one is an answer to the question, "What is marriage for?" This is going to take a bit, so settle in. We'll talk about friendship, then gardening, then sexuality, and then family. Here we go ...

Uno: Friendship

After he created Adam, God said, "It is not good for the man to be alone."[1]

Why not?

Well, because humans are made in God's image. That means we are called to image God, to mirror and mimic God to the world. But that's a problem for Adam because God exists in a web of life-giving relationships, but Adam is alone.

Early in the story, God says, "Let *us* make mankind in *our* image."[2] Who is God talking to? Himself![3]

Later in Scripture Jesus talks about God as the "Father," the "Son," and the "Spirit." But at this point in the story all we know is that *God is not alone.* And if God is not alone, why should Adam be?

I cannot tell you how often I hear people say, "All you need is God." That makes for nice song lyrics, but the problem is, it's just not true. God never says, "All you need is God." Adam *has* God, and it's not enough. God says, "It is not good for the man to be alone"!

Now, that doesn't mean you have to get married. There are other avenues for up-close, vulnerable relationships. Jesus was single (sorry, Dan Brown). For Jesus' followers, singleness can be an amazing way to live. The Christian tradition is filled with men and women who never married, yet found life-giving friendships. But I'm married. It's what I know. And in my personal experience, marriage is an eye-opening glimpse into the inner workings of God.

In the wedding ceremony God says, "They become one flesh." That word *one* is *echad* in Hebrew. It's a graphic, weighty word. When you combine it with the word *flesh*, it basically means "fused together at the deepest levels." And the *exact same word* is used for God. The ancient Hebrews had a prayer called the *Shema* that was the epicenter of Israel's faith — "Hear, O Israel: the LORD our God, the LORD is *echad*."[4] *God* is fused together at the deepest levels. And in marriage we catch glimpses, hints, shadows of that kind of oneness.

There's a line in the Hebrew wisdom literature that refers to a person's spouse as his or her *allup.*[5] It's a word that can be translated "companion" or "best friend."

Your spouse is your closest friend.

That's one of the reasons God created marriage. For you to walk through life with the person you enjoy. With your spouse as the primary relationship in your life. Your *allup*. The one who knows you better than anybody. Better than your own mother.

To know and be known is a powerful thing. My wife knows all my flaws — trust me, there are many — and she *still* loves me. She still wants to get coffee and go for a walk. She still wants to spend her day off with me. This is one of my favorite things about my wife, hands down.

She's my friend.

There's nothing like waking up in the morning next to Tammy, knowing she's in my corner.

No matter what the day throws at me, I know I'm not alone.

Dos: Gardening

God put Adam in the garden to "work it and take care of it." That was a part of human's job description. The not-alone God says, "Let us make mankind in our image, in our likeness, *so that they may rule* ..."[6]

Then God says, "Be fruitful and increase in number; fill the earth and subdue it. *Rule* over the fish in the sea and the birds in the sky and over every living creature that moves on the ground."[7]

Human was created to rule over the earth and subdue it. So let's take a minute to hash this out.

The Hebrew word translated "rule" means to actively partner with God in taking the world somewhere. And the word *subdue* doesn't mean to exploit or harm the earth. It means to harness the raw materials that make up the planet, all that pent-up potentiality, and make something beautiful.

In the modern world we call that "work." And work gets a bad rap. In fact, a lot of people think work is a part of the curse. Nothing could be further from the truth! *Toil* is a part of the curse. Thorns in the ground are a part of the curse. Sweat and blood and ibuprofen are a part of the curse. But work is a part of the original Edenic creation.

We were created to work. But not just any kind of work. To work for human flourishing. To partner with God to make a gardenlike world in which humans can thrive and God can walk with his people in the cool of the day. What the Hebrews called *shalom*.

Contrary to the mantra of the day, we do not work to live. In God's economy, we live to work.

Yet, so many people *do* work to live. The goal is to make as much money as possible with as little effort as possible so they can get "off work" and go enjoy life. In the words of a 1980s one-hit wonder, "Everybody's working for the weekend ..."

Really? What a miserable way to live.

Instead, we need to recapture a theology of vocation. The word *vocation* comes from a Latin word meaning "calling." I believe there is a calling on every person's life to partner with God in their corner of the garden and to work for human flourishing.

I believe God calls pastors like myself, and God calls architects and artists and accountants and stay-at-home moms and baristas and mortgage brokers — and on down the list. We need the full spectrum of vocations for Eden — not just "spiritual" vocations (whatever that means), but every human on the planet doing what God made them to do.

The *first thing* God does with Adam is put him in the garden to "work it and take care of it."

Everybody needs a gardening project.

Put another way, everybody needs to find a calling in life. A sense of, "This is what I was put on earth to do. This is what I'm good at. This is what I was made for. This is my Eden, my corner of the earth to rule over."

What's your calling? What's your gardening project? You need to be able to answer that question, or in time the wheels will fall off in your marriage. Why? Because *all healthy marriages are built around a calling*. Marriage is a means to an end. It exists for friendship, yes, but also to partner with God for the remaking of shalom.

Couples who exist simply for one another are doomed to failure.

If the point of your marriage is *your marriage*, it will collapse in on itself.

If the end goal of your relationship is *your relationship*, it will self-destruct.

You can only sit at a coffee shop and stare into each other's eyes for so long. At some point you have to get up and *do* something. That's why — in an ideal world — you should have a sense of your calling *before* you get married. And the marriage should be built around that calling.

Now, I know this raises as many questions as it does answers. What if you're not sure about your vocation? What if your vocation changes over the years? What if your spouse's vocation is out of sync with your own? What if you're in school, and you're years away from living out your vocation? These are all great questions, but they are beyond the scope of this book. For now, here's what I'm trying to say. Marriage is a means to an end. It exists for something larger than itself.

That's what we see in the beginning.

Adam was called by God to take care of Eden. But it was too much work for one man. Eden was massive.[8] Adam was incapable of gardening the whole thing. He needed help.

That's why God created Eve. God says, "I will make him a helper suitable for him."

The word *helper* is *ezer* in Hebrew. It sounds derogatory in English, like God made Adam a personal assistant. But it's not that way at all in the original language. *Ezer* can be translated "partner" — one who comes alongside to help achieve a goal.

The exact same word is used for God in *Psalms*. The psalmist sings, "The LORD is with me; he is my *helper*."[9] In other places it's used of military reinforcements without which an army would be crushed.

A helper is *not* an employee — someone who works for you, someone you boss around.

A helper is an equal. *Genesis* uses the adjective *suitable*, meaning "on the same level." It's someone you love and respect. And it's one who comes alongside as a partner in a project, as an ally in a war. We all need that kind of helper. Or put another way, *we all need help.*

Women, don't marry a man without a gardening project.

No matter how charming or romantic or handsome or spontaneous or stylish he is, if he isn't a gardener, how will you "respect" him?[10]

If he isn't doing anything with his life that matters for God's kingdom, how will you partner with him? If he isn't going anywhere, how will you follow him? If his life is just about the day-to-day kind of pleasures, how will you entrust your future and *your* calling to him?

Men, don't marry a woman who doesn't want to be your *ezer,* your partner in life.

No matter how smart or sexy or funny or interesting she is, if she doesn't want to help you in kingdom work, how will your marriage be about more than your marriage? If she doesn't believe in you, how will you ever trust her? If she doesn't want to follow God's calling on your marriage, how will you dream, try, fail, and succeed with her? How will you leave the world a better place than you found it?

If you ignore this and get into a marriage with no sense of calling, it's only a matter of time until you start thinking, "What now? What's next?" It's implanted into your humanness. God created marriage for you to do something. To put on your gloves, pick up your shovels, and, hand in hand, go make a world.

Tres: Sexuality

The last line in the story is, "Adam and his wife were both naked, and they felt no shame."[11]

Two young, amorous, naked people in a garden. Sounds like reality TV gone bad, but it's actually the first love story in the Scriptures.

They were friends, yes, and they were partners as well, but they were also lovers.

God created the human body. *All* of the human body. And not one part is by accident. I doubt God saw Adam and Eve messing around in the garden and thought, "What the heck! That's not what those are for!"

Your sexuality is a part of your humanity. We're going to talk more about this in a while, but for now, know that for most people, the body is one-half of an equation. It's incomplete.

It's a band without a drummer.

A sentence without a …

That's by design. God made you that way on purpose. To share your sexuality with another human being.

God created marriage as the context for your sexuality. And the inverse is also true. He created sexuality as the glue to hold marriage together. More on that later.

For now, know that if you want to get married in order to have sex, that's not bad or shallow or selfish. As long as it's not the *only* reason you want to get married. Because sex is one of the reasons God thought up this adventure called marriage.

Have at it!

Cuatro: Family

Now, Adam and Eve lived a long time ago. Long before condoms and birth control. Which means it wasn't long before Adam and Eve became Adam and Eve and Cain ... and Abel ... and Seth ... and "other sons and daughters."[12] (On a side note, how would you like to be the "other sons and daughters"? Lame.)

This was by design. In fact, God said, "Be fruitful and increase in number; fill the earth ..."[13]

Did you know that's actually the first command in the entire Bible? God *commands* the original humans to make babies.

I like this God.

He's a God who is really into the family. In *Genesis*, family is the building block of society as a whole. Throughout the Scriptures, God is called "Father," and we are called "sons and daughters" and "brothers and sisters." Family is at the heart of God's vision for the world.

We live in a culture that can err on one of two sides.

One camp doesn't want kids at all. Sex, sure. Marriage, maybe. Family? No way. The cycle for millions of relationships is "hook up, shack up, break up." And children are collateral damage.

More than one-fifth of all pregnancies in the United States end in abortion.[14]

One out of three kids goes to bed without a dad.[15]

The number of children born out of wedlock to women under thirty is more than 50 percent in most of the country.[16]

In this way of thinking, children are seen as a nuisance, and family as a hindrance to "freedom." This is so very far from God's heart.

Another camp idolizes children. I see this in the church all the time. We emphasize family so much that it becomes a weird kind of idol. Young couples can't walk three feet without somebody asking them, "When are you going to have kids?" The subliminal message is if you don't have kids, you're not in the club.

This isn't just a problem in the church. It's all over the place. When people don't find life in God, they start to look for it elsewhere, and family is a natural place to start. Kids become gods. Parenting becomes tantamount to a religion. The parents exist to make the children happy. And all too often the marriage is sacrificed on the altar of child-centered parenting. We've all seen it—the family falling out of the minivan; the haggard mom; the detached, frustrated father; the kids running wild. You think to yourself, "That will *never* happen to me."

That's not what God had in mind.

Rather, family exists to spread God's rule out over the earth. If we're going to "fill the earth and subdue it," it's going to take more than one man, more than one marriage, and more than one family. It's going to take all of the human race.

That doesn't mean everyone needs to get married or all married couples need to have kids. Some can't. And there are other ways to live out that calling. But it does mean family is one of the reasons God created marriage.

. . .

There you have it. That's the *why*. The point of it all. The reason you walk down the aisle, stand up in front of your family and friends, and give your life away to another human being, "as long as you both shall live." Are you getting the picture? Is it coming into focus? Can you pick up the tone and depth and color? Marriage is about so much more than marriage. Adam and Eve weren't made to just sit around and chat. They were made to do life together, to work and sweat and bleed for a better world, to make love whenever they wanted, and in the end to "be fruitful and increase in number" so this experience can go on and on and on. At least, that's what we see in the beginning.

But there's a problem. We don't live in the garden anymore ...

Reverse engineering, "the one," and other things — like unicorns

Genesis 2 ends with, "Adam and his wife were both naked, and they felt no shame." Two humans, wrapped up in a relationship for life, centered around friendship, gardening, sexuality, and family. It was beautiful.

And short-lived. Oh, how I wish Genesis 2 were the end of the story. Life would be so much easier. But there's no getting around Genesis 3.

In the following story, Eve is tempted by the serpent. She's called to rule *over* the creation, but instead she's ruled *by* the creation. It's a sad turn of events — an upending of the created order.

The first place sin wreaks havoc is in Adam and Eve's relationship. God says to Adam, "Have you eaten from the tree that I commanded you not to eat from?"[1]

Adam fires back, "The woman you put here with me — she gave me some fruit from the tree." Nice. Not only does he sound like a six-year-old, but he blames it all on his wife.

Eve goes on the defensive. "The serpent deceived me."

And just like that, the first marriage is infected by the disease.

Blame shifting.

Obstinate hearts.

Anger.

Distance.

Regret.

And we are the sons of Adam and the daughters of Eve. We live in the wake of our first parents' misstep. Because we are just as screwed up as they were, all marriages face tension. Some more than others, but nobody is immune. We all suffer from the garden tragedy.

We're a long, long way from Eden.

But there's good news. Jesus' agenda is to fix it. *All* of it.

Cinco: re-creation

The New Testament is filled with language that echoes Genesis 1 and 2. Take *The Gospel of John*. The opening line is, "In the beginning was the Word ... Through him all things were made."[2] John is retelling the story of creation. He's saying that a *new* creation is coming to birth in and through "the Word"—his name for Jesus. To John, the gospel is about the re-creation. Of what? Everything.

I think of Paul's letter to the church in Colossae. "God was pleased to have all his fullness dwell in him [Jesus], and through him to reconcile to himself all things, whether things on earth or things in heaven, by making peace through his blood, shed on the cross."[3] Wow. I need to catch my breath after reading that.

God is going to put the whole cosmos back into the shape he intended "in the beginning," and here's the salient point — *he's starting with you and me.*

There's a line in Paul's letter to the Jesus followers in Corinth in which he writes, "If anyone is in Christ, the new creation has come: The old has gone, the new is here!"[4]

If you're a follower of Jesus, then you are a new creation.

You don't live in the garden anymore, true. You were made in the image of God, and sin fractured that image, but it's still there. Latent in your humanity. And the Spirit of Jesus is at work in your life. He's re-creating you from the ground up.

But keep in mind that creation is a process, not an item on a to-do list. And the creative process takes time. A lot of time. What you and I call "the creative process," theologians call "sanctification." Don't get scared off by the technical jargon. To be sanctified means "to be set apart" from the ugly, distorted human you used to be and remade into the real you.

Get that. The *real* you.

To God, your identity — what makes you *you* — isn't rooted in the past (who you were) or in the present (who you are), but in the future — in who you are becoming.[5]

That's why Paul can say things like, "You are holy." In fact, the New Testament writings call you by all kinds of lofty language — holy, dearly loved, pure, blameless, chosen, children of God, co-heirs with Messiah Jesus, etc.[6]

Me? Are you sure? Yes.

In theology this is called "eschatological realism," which is a way of saying *you are in the process of becoming who you really are.*

You are "holy," and you are in the process of becoming holy.

You are "pure," and you are in the process of becoming pure.

You are "blameless" (or without defect), and you are in the process of becoming blameless.

God starts with the end in mind and works backward, kind of like reverse engineering. I think of Paul's language to the church in Ephesus. "Live a life worthy of the calling you have received."[7] Put another way, "This is who you are. Now live up to it."

What does this have to do with marriage? A lot.

For starters, it blows up the idea of "the one." The long-standing urban legend that there is a mythical creature out there somewhere (probably next to a unicorn) who was made to "complete" you. Your "missing half." Is that true? Let's put this question to bed once and for all.

No.

This idea doesn't come from the Scriptures, not even close. It comes from Greek mythology, specifically from an ancient writing by Plato called the *Symposium*.[8] According to Plato, humans were originally androgynous, each one with four arms, four legs, two sets of genitalia (male and female), and one head made up of two faces.

Picture *that*. Sounds like something out of a film by Guillermo del Toro.

These four-legged, two-faced humans became a threat to the gods, but the pantheon didn't want to destroy them. If they did, they would lose their worship (which is such a pain). So Zeus, the king of the gods, split humans in two, cutting their strength in half and doubling the number of worshipers. Smart guy.

Plato writes that ever since then, we've been searching for our "missing half." As if you were separated in the past but out there somewhere is the one who will "complete" you.

The story of God is very different, and so much better. (No offense to the ancient Greeks.) There is no such thing as "the one." You don't have a missing half, and you're not incomplete. In reality, marriage is two broken people coming together to find healing in Jesus. And one broken person plus another broken person does not equal bliss! The math adds up in the opposite direction — twice as much brokenness.

And guess what? That's a good thing. Because the friction in a marriage exposes all the places where God is still at work in us. That's a gift. Not only that, but in the wake of the fall, that's one of the reasons for marriage — re-creation.

The point of marriage isn't to find our missing half. It's to help each other become all that God intended. Our future, real selves. In marriage, two people partner to that end. They see the best in each other — the person God created them to be — and they push and pull each other toward that goal.

Don't get married because you think he or she is "the one." Trust me, they're not. There's no such thing! But *do* get married when you see who God is making somebody to be, and it lights you up. When you want to be a part of that story of transformation. That journey to the future. When you are well aware it will be a long and bumpy ride, but you don't want to miss one mile. Because you believe in God's calling on them, and you want in.

My wife makes me a better person. She calls out the best in me. She calls me to live up to who I really am, to who God is making me to be.

She also brings out the *worst* in me. What Paul calls "the flesh."[9]

The ugly, nasty part of me that doesn't want to change. She exposes my selfishness and my pride.

That's why marriage is humbling. I thought I was a pretty decent guy — and then I got married. Turns out I'm kind of a toolshed. It's easy to be a decent guy when you live in a bubble. But when you step into marriage, your true colors bleed out. It's like squeezing a sponge. Whatever is on the inside comes out, for better or for worse.

If there are serious problems in your life, don't expect them to go away when you get married. Usually they get worse.

If you struggle with pornography now, marriage probably won't stop that. If you are insecure now, don't expect a husband or wife to fix that. If you're not happy being single, trust me, the odds are you won't be happy being married. That's how it works. Marriage will expose what's already inside you.

I can be brash and inconsiderate. My mouth gets me in trouble all the time. I do life with a community of about a dozen people.[10] We all live close to each other, spend gobs of time together, and live out the gospel in our neighborhood. Because of that, we know each other really, really well. Once a week we share a meal together and then break into groups of three or four to pray over each other. Just the other day I said, "Guys, whenever you see sin in my life, I want you to call me out. Open-door policy. Please tell me." And sure enough, *right then and there*, they all said, "The way you speak to your wife isn't okay. You need to put a filter on your mouth." They were right. I get frustrated and upset, and it leaks out in sarcastic digs. So messed up. My brothers are now praying for me to change, and I know Jesus is at work in all this, but it's not an overnight fix. Thank God my wife is patient.

Tammy sees the real me. The future me, the John Mark I am becoming. And she, like my community, *and like my God*, calls me forward into that reality. And I'd like to think I do the same for her. Because I believe in her, and in who God is making her to be. We help each other become our real, true selves.

Tammy is a guardrail, a yellow line in the middle of my windshield, a signpost pointing forward to my destination. It's not a smooth or straight road, but there's no way I'm going back.

Happy

Well, that's the gist of it.

Friendship.

Gardening.

Sexuality.

Family.

That's why you get married. That's why God created marriage. And in the wake of the fall, a fifth reason is added — *re-creation*.

Here's the problem — that's not why most people get married.

At least, that's not why I got married. I got married to be happy. Don't get me wrong. I was into all that other stuff. She was my closest friend. There was a calling on our life together that we were excited about. Sex ... uh ... *yes*. And we both wanted a family one day. But none of those reasons were *the* reason.

Like millions upon millions of other Americans, I married for happiness.

That sounds innocuous at first glance. Heck, it sounds romantic. But the trouble is that happiness is the *result* of a healthy marriage. It's not the *reason* for marriage. Happiness is a great thing, but it's the by-product, the afterclap of marriage. It's not the point.

God doesn't look down on Adam and say, "He looks sad. He needs a lift. He needs another human being to quench the thirst of his soul. I will make him a helper to satisfy his deepest longings. Eve, the pressure's on." Of course not. Only God can do that.

A spouse is not a substitute for God.

I cringe when I'm at a wedding where the guy says, "I promise to make you happy." I want to stand up and scream, "You can't keep that promise. It's impossible. You aren't God!"

Is it any wonder that the number-one justification for divorce is "I deserve to be happy"? If you put your faith in your spouse to make you happy, it's only a matter of time until they let you down.

Our whole mind-set on happiness is deeply flawed. "I *deserve* to be happy." Really? I'm not sure that's right. All of life is a gift from the Creator God. We think we have the right to "life, liberty, and the pursuit of happiness." But contrary to what the American propaganda machine says, happiness is not a right. It's a gift. God doesn't owe you anything. And neither does your spouse. It's all a gift.

You *have* to get this before you get married. Sadly, I didn't, and it caused me so much pain. Not to mention how it hurt my wife.

If you go into marriage searching for happiness, all you will do is walk out filled with disillusionment. Don't get me wrong. Marriage is incredible! But it's not heaven on earth. It's two broken people coming together to follow God's calling on their lives.

Let marriage be marriage, and let God be God. Let marriage be for friendship and gardening and sex and family and re-creation. And let God be the well for your soul. Your source of life.

This doesn't mean you won't be happy in marriage. I am. Most of the best memories of my life have Tammy attached to them. The night I lost my virginity, our honeymoon in Europe, moving to Portland, starting a church, the birth of our first child, that vacation in Kauai — we did all of that *together*. And it was fun. If I were to edit her out of my story, it would be flat, anemic, and boring. Here's what I've learned over the last few years. God is the source of my life, not Tammy. She's an amazing gift that I don't deserve, but she's not Jesus. It took me a long time to get this. And to be honest, I'm still pounding away on living it out. Hopefully, you'll get this sooner than I did. Because the beauty of this way of living is that if and when happiness shows up on your doorstep, it's icing on the cake.

Part 3
Sex

Very good

"God saw all that he had made, and it was very good."

So ends the creation story in Genesis 1. In the original language, the closing line is melodic. It has a rhythm to it. It's like God is singing over his brand-new world — *it is very good.*

I love that word *good*. In Hebrew, it's the word *tov*, and it has to do with the human senses — taste, touch, smell, sight, and sound.

In the Scriptures, *tov* is used of bread, wine, honey, lotion, perfume, fruit, a feast, a home, and the shade under a tree on a hot Middle Eastern day. It can be translated "pleasing" or "lovely" or "beautiful."

The taste of fresh, well-made food in your mouth is *tov.*

The smell of crisp, alpine air when you're out hiking is *tov.*

The sight of a beautiful woman is *tov.*

And *sex* is *tov.*

God saw *all* that he had made. Everything in the created order. The sand on the beach, and the sunset on the horizon. The sound of music. Food and drink. The human body. And everything we call "sex." Beauty, attraction, the desire of lovers, touch, arousal, foreplay, the joy of a kiss on your mouth, the orgasm — it's *all* good.

In fact, sex is *very* good.

What does this say about God? We have a tendency to think of God as austere and stoic. As if God's a grumpy old man who is mad at the world and doesn't want anybody to have fun. But nothing could be further from the truth.

God is a God of pleasure.

We see this in Jesus. He's always "eating and drinking" — so much so that he was called a "glutton and a drunkard" by his critics.[1] One of my favorite things about Jesus is he's always up for a free meal. In the second chapter of *The Gospel of John*, we find Jesus at a wedding, having a great time, when all of a sudden the host runs out of wine. To me, that's not a big deal, but in first-century Eastern culture, that was a serious problem. Hospitality was paramount at a wedding, and the host was expected to have more than enough wine for all the guests. That's when Jesus, after a bit of arm-twisting from his mother, steps in and turns water into wine.

Now, that's my kind of miracle.

To wrap up the story, John writes, "What Jesus did here in Cana of Galilee was the first of the signs through which he revealed his glory."

Is that how you think of God's "glory"? Water into wine?

Is that how you envision Jesus? At a wedding, glass in hand, with a smile on his lips?

That's what God is like. He's a God of pleasure—he was in the beginning, and over the millennia nothing has changed. I love Paul's line in *1 Timothy* about how God "richly provides us with everything for our enjoyment."[2]

We need a theology of enjoyment, not just when we talk about sex, but when we talk about the rest of life.[3] A *Genesis*-shaped world-view that says, "This world was created by God. He enjoys it, and so should we." And we need to enjoy creation as an act of worship.

All of it. Including sex. Richard Foster once said, "Sex, at its best, at its highest, at its holiest, is play."[4] He's right. Sex is about pro-creation, and it's about recreation. It turns out that "be fruitful and increase in number" is a really fun command to obey.

Both my wife and I were virgins when we married. Our first night as a married couple was *so much fun*. Of course it was awkward and clumsy and a bit embarrassing too, but it was unforgettable. I had never seen a naked woman before, much less put my hands on one. And to do so with my best friend and the woman of my dreams was, and still is, an incredible experience.

We honeymooned in the UK, and for the first week we stayed in a hotel right on Hyde Park in London. Our first night we walked across the park to catch a show at the Royal Albert Hall. *Romeo and Juliet*. About halfway through the play, during the über-depressing part, my wife turned to me and whispered, "Wanna get outta here and go make love?" The answer to that question is *always* yes. We snuck out the back, and, well, our son Jude is seven.

I will never forget thinking about God that night as my wife and I were lying in bed — about the fact that God created sex and that what I was enjoying was all his idea.

That's what *tov* does. It makes us step back, breathe it all in, and well up with gratitude to the God who is that generous. Because we realize it's all a gift.

The very first "commandment" in the Bible is "be fruitful and increase in number."[5] That's strange language for us. We don't talk about sex that way anymore because with the advent of contraceptives, we've disconnected sex from procreation. We say "make love" or "sleep together" or "have sex." But it's the same idea. And it's the first command out of God's mouth.

For too long, however, the church's message on sex has been reduced to "don't!"

"Don't view porn."

"Don't masturbate."

"Don't make out."

"Don't sleep around."

"Don't sleep together before you get married."

And all of that is true. But the problem is that the Scriptures don't start with a negative command about sex — "Don't." They start with a positive command — "Be fruitful and increase in number."

One of the first things we read about Adam and Eve is that they "were both naked, and they felt no shame." Can you imagine sex with no guilt or shame? Nothing to hide? Just pure, unadulterated joy between a man and a woman, locked into relationship for life. *That* is what God created.

And notice that all of this is before the fall. We were sexual *before* we were sinful.[6] Sex is not an evil curse we have to curb and deny. It's a good gift we get to enjoy, as long as it's in the right context.

We don't think this way anymore — at least not in the Western church. We have been deeply shaped by dualism. That's the idea that the "spiritual world" (whatever that means) is good and the "physical world" is evil. But because we live in the physical world, dualism causes us to carry around a heaping dose of guilt. Every time we experience *tov*, we feel a twinge of shame. As if we're not supposed to get pleasure from the world but must just endure it and wait for an escape to a place called "heaven," which is very far away from the world we inhabit now. That's not what the Scriptures teach, but many of us think this way.

This deviant worldview is all over the place. Think about how we pray over a meal. We ask God to "bless the food." What a strange thing to pray. A lot of people claim we pray before meals because of Jesus. After all, there's this story in *The Gospel of Matthew* where Jesus blessed the food right before feeding thousands of people.[7] But that's not quite true. Read the story. It says he "gave thanks." That's different. A first-century Jew would never bless the food.[8] It's already blessed! In fact, it *is* the blessing. A first-century Jewish rabbi like Jesus would *bless God* for the food.

Blessing the food is a later interpolation. In the Middle Ages, when Plato's voice started to drown out Jesus' and dualism began to infect the church, Christians started blessing the food. They started to believe that the physical world was evil, and since they were about to get pleasure from the physical world, they had to ask for "grace."

That's why Christians, at least in America, pray before the meal, but orthodox Jews pray *after* the meal—as a way of saying thank you to the Creator. Oddly enough, orthodox Jews don't believe Jesus is the Messiah, but in this area their worldview is much closer to Jesus' than to the worldviews of many Christians.

Now, here's my point: This dualistic worldview bleeds into how we think about sex. So much so that the church's message on sex can essentially be reduced to this dualistic slogan. "Sex is dirty—save it for the one you love."

We would never voice that sentiment out loud, but far too often it is the subliminal message from the church. For example, to be a Catholic priest, you have to be celibate. Now, I have nothing but respect for a man (or woman) who would give up sex in order to serve God, and my Catholic brothers in the priesthood are doing incredible things all around the world, but sometimes they can give off an underlying feeling that sex is somehow unspiritual.[9] And this isn't just a Catholic thing. I think of the stereotypical youth pastor who tells his kids that sex is sinful and evil and it will wreck them forever, and then turns around and tells them to save it for marriage. What?

That is such a damaging way to think about sex. It's so far from the heart of God. Yes, we live in a cracked world, and sex is abused right and left, but that doesn't mean sex itself is bad. Even after the fall, God's view of sex as a good gift is unchanged.

There's more than one garden

In the Hebrew wisdom literature, there's this book called *Song of Songs*. It's an ancient collection of erotic Jewish love poetry. And it's in the Bible. Orthodox Jewish males aren't allowed to read *The Song* until the age of thirty. If you're an Orthodox Jewish guy, uh, I'm sorry ...

For a long time, people have been trying to turn *The Song* into an allegory of some kind. The idea of a racy love poem in the Bible makes the dualist cringe. And so over the years people have been trying to make *The Song* into something less ... explicit. As a result, lots of people read it as a "picture" of Jesus and the church. So *lips* don't really mean lips. *Kissing* doesn't really mean kissing. And—obviously—*breasts* don't really mean breasts. It's about "spiritual" stuff.

Years ago, I sat through a sermon in which a pastor read the verse, "Your breasts are like two fawns ... that browse among the lilies." He said, "The left breast symbolizes the Old Testament. The right breast symbolizes the New. And in between is the cross." Uh ... no. First, that's weird. Second, I think the poet just means he likes her breasts. Why can't we just read it as the author intended?

With all due respect, I don't think *The Song* is an allegory.[10] I read it as a celebration of love between a king and a shepherd girl, and it's highly sexual.[11] Chapter 4 is actually a sex scene. We read about a man and a woman on their wedding night. She's undressing, and he's writing about her body, from the top down.

He starts off with her eyes ...

> How beautiful you are, my darling!
>> Oh how beautiful!
>> Your eyes behind your veil are doves ...

Then, after her hair and teeth—her lips ...

> Your lips are like a scarlet ribbon;
>> your mouth is lovely ...

Then her neck and breasts ...

> Your neck is like the tower of David,
>   built with courses of stone;
> on it hang a thousand shields,
>   all of them shields of warriors.
> Your breasts are like two fawns,
>   like twin fawns of a gazelle
>   that browse among the lilies.

After that, his language is poetic, but if you use your imagination, you'll figure out what he's saying ...

> Until the day breaks
>   and the shadows flee,
> I will go to the mountain of myrrh
>   and to the hill of incense.

Whenever I read this out loud, people laugh. "Your neck is like the tower of David." Really? In what century was that *ever* a compliment? We don't live in an agrarian society, and the organic, earthy language sounds odd to us. But it's actually genius. The poet is able to invoke highly sexual imagery without ever sounding crass.

A few stanzas later he says this ...

> You are a garden locked up, my sister, my bride;
>   you are a spring enclosed, a sealed fountain.

That's an ancient way of saying she's a virgin. A fountain was a euphemism for a woman's sexuality. She's a "sealed fountain," not easy to get into. But she's anything but a prude. She's an eager participant in this evocative scene, saying to her lover ...

> Awake, north wind,
>> and come, south wind!
> Blow on my garden,
>> that its fragrance may spread everywhere.
> Let my beloved come into his garden
>> and taste its choice fruits.

After a time of foreplay, she's inviting her new husband to come into "his garden." Listen to the next line ...

> I have come into my garden, my sister, my bride;
>> I have gathered my myrrh with my spice.
> I have eaten my honeycomb and my honey;
>> I have drunk my wine and my milk.

This is the couple lying in bed after it's over. Reveling in the pleasure of the moment. It's the incredible feeling you get after sex. You feel release, calm, at peace. You feel close, intimate, safe—and in marriage, you feel "naked and unashamed." It's *such* a great feeling.

But the story isn't quite done. It ends with an interjection.[12] A voice from outside speaks over the lovers ...

> Eat, friends, and drink;
>> drink your fill of love.

The question is, who's the voice? The two lovers are alone in the bedroom, so who is speaking?

God is.

(And no, that is not a misprint.)

God says, "Drink your fill of love."

How crazy is that? The maker of the stars is singing over two naked lovers on their wedding night.

Does that sound anything like dualism to you? Not at all. This God's view of sex is incredible. Even in an off-kilter world, with so much pain and regret and wounding from sexuality gone awry, God is still singing over the good gift he created. From creation, through the fall, to the shattered world we now call home, and over all the noise, he's still singing, "It is *very* good."

Gifts become gods

Sadly, like everything else God created, sex can be defaced. Graffiti can adhere to any surface.

Ever since the garden, we've been mistaking the good creation for the even better creator. Eve saw that the fruit was "pleasing to the eye,"[13] and she chose the taste of food over the presence of God. She chose the creation over the creator. And her children are born with the exact same slant.

Think of the story of the Israelites in the desert. God rescued his people out of slavery in Egypt, but before the Israelites left, they asked the Egyptians for "articles of silver and gold." Moses writes, "The LORD had made the Egyptians favorably disposed toward the people, and they gave them what they asked for; so they plundered the Egyptians." [14]

I love that. Dirt-poor slaves became wealthy overnight. Men and women with nothing to call their own walked out of Egypt with silver and gold. A nation that had known nothing but oppression for hundreds of years was set free in a day. And all this was from the hand of God.

Yet all too soon they traded freedom for slavery again. A few months later, Moses was up on Mount Sinai getting the Ten Commandments. He was gone for a while, and the people started to get antsy. They said to Aaron, "Come, make us gods who will go before us. As for this fellow Moses who brought us up out of Egypt, we don't know what has happened to him." [15]

The next part of the story is fascinating. Aaron caved. He said, "Take off the gold earrings that your wives, your sons and your daughters are wearing, and bring them to me … He took what they handed him and made it into an idol cast in the shape of a calf, fashioning it with a tool. Then they said, 'These are your gods, Israel, who brought you up out of Egypt.'"

Where did they get the gold earrings? *From the Egyptians!* Or, to be more precise, from God. It was God who moved the Egyptians to be "favorably disposed" toward the Israelites. They made an idol out of the very thing that was a gift from God.

Are we any different?

There is a bent in all of us to turn gifts into gods.

After all, we're hard-wired for worship. Don't think for one second that worship is a religious thing. No, worship is a *human* thing. Religious people worship, yes — and so do agnostics and atheists. We all make something ultimate. We all make sacrifices. Every one of us gives our life away to something or someone greater than ourselves. The novelist David Foster Wallace, a few years before he committed suicide, said, "Everybody worships. The only choice we get is *what* to worship."[16]

We were made to worship God, but sin bends us in the direction of idolatry. We have a slant to take God's gifts and make them into wannabe gods.

Sex is no exception. In *Romans*, Paul writes, "God gave them over in the sinful desires of their hearts to sexual impurity for the degrading of their bodies with one another. They exchanged the truth about God for a lie, *and worshiped and served created things rather than the Creator.*"[17]

Paul's first example of idolatry is sex. That's telling.

In Paul's day, the goddess of sexuality was called Aphrodite. Paul spent a few years in her hometown, Ephesus, getting a church up and running right under her nose. We have writings from the ancient Greeks saying the temple in Ephesus was stacked with one thousand temple prostitutes. *One thousand!* People would come to Ephesus from all over the world to "worship" with one of the prostitutes (i.e., have sex with someone they barely know). Sound at all familiar?

Aphrodite is alive and well.

Today she's the CEO of a multibillion dollar global industry. Entertainment, television, marketing, porn, strip clubs, fashion, cosmetics, health, fitness, plastic surgery, Botox, Viagra — her temple is ubiquitous.

And she's not easy to please. She demands we make sacrifices. We have to give up our innocence, our purity, often our body's well-being, and, of course, our freedom. Because when we turn sex into a god, it becomes a cruel tyrant. What is supposed to function as a gift for us to enjoy becomes an addiction with a strange, otherworldly power over us.

That's one of the crazy things about my generation. More than any other in the history of the world, this generation values the freedom of the individual. The sexual revolution of the 1960s made sexual freedom a "right," and "keep your laws off my body" is the mantra of the day.

We're just now learning that what looks like freedom is actually slavery.

When sex is your god, you *have* to download porn. You *have* to jack off. You *have* to sleep with your boyfriend. You *have* to let him touch you. You *have* to give into your body's cravings, even if you know it's going to steal from your future. You have no choice because you're a slave.

We like to define freedom as the ability to do whatever we want, whenever we want, with whomever we want. But to Jesus, that's not freedom—that's slavery! Freedom, at least in Jesus' mind, is the ability to do whatever you *should*. To enjoy the world as God intended. To live fully awake and alive.

That's why the message about Jesus is good news. Because *Jesus* is king, not Aphrodite. He has the power to sweep the legs out from under every Pharaoh on earth. In him we can live free. It was Jesus who said, "You will know the truth, *and the truth will set you free.*" [18]

My prayer for my generation is that we will find freedom in the saving power of Jesus.

Freedom from the carnage and pain caused by sex when it's torn out of God's hands.

Freedom to healing and a clean slate.

Freedom from the cynicism many feel toward sex and from the allure many have to her power.

And freedom to see sex as a gift. Nothing less, and nothing more. Not as a dirty secret to be swept under the rug and not as a god to be worshiped, but as a gift, and a good one at that.

Maybe sex for you is baggage and pain and regret and dread. I want you to hear that sex is *tov*. It's good. And Jesus wants to heal the way you think about sexuality.

Or maybe for you sex is *everything*, a god of sorts. It's what you're chasing after, thinking that if you can just get close enough, you'll find life. But it's not going to happen. If you make sex a god, it will not only enslave you. It will let you down. As incredible as sex is, it can't live up to all the hype. At least not for long. If you put it on a pedestal, you'll find it's made of balsa wood.

Think of all the mystery and allure and buzz that the world puts on sex. Think of how it's portrayed in film — spontaneous, wild, orgasmic, thrilling. And it can be all of those things — *sometimes*. But even then, it's not God.

It was never supposed to be.

From the beginning, sex was a means to an end. A gift to push you to something even better.

Echad

I'm six foot two with long arms and tall legs. I speak in public for a living, and one of the first things I hear when I meet people after a gathering is, "You're so much taller in real life." I'm not sure what people mean by that, but because I'm insecure I take it to mean I look short and fat on stage.

And what does "in real life" mean?

Then a few weeks ago, I was asked by three different people why I tan, wear makeup, and put highlights in my hair. (To set the record straight, I don't tan — I take vitamin D. I *don't* wear makeup. And the highlights are natural. I swear.)

So, from offstage I guess I look like a short, overweight dude who wears makeup, tans, and thinks blond highlights are still all the rage.

The dream of the '90s is alive in Portland.

I think the reason I feel so weird about my body is because, well, it's my body. There's this pervasive idea right now that the "real you" is on the inside — like your body is just a shell to carry "you" around. We live in a culture that is obsessed with body image, and it breeds insecurity. After all, how many of us look like the collage of images we see in the media every day?

So people overreact and say things like, "You need to love me for *me*, not my body." There's some truth in that, for sure, but I don't think I buy the logic. It's a false dichotomy. Your body and the "real you" are interconnected. You can't split it apart like that.

What if I said, "You need to love me for *me*, not my personality." You would think, "What? But your personality is a part of who you are."

Exactly.

From the dust of the ground

When God made human, he made a unique creature, unlike any other in the universe. The author of *Genesis* writes, "The LORD God formed a man from the dust of the ground and breathed into his nostrils the breath of life, and the man became a living being."[1]

The word *man* is *adam* in Hebrew, from which we get the name Adam. And there's a play on words in the text. *Adam*, the man, is made from the *adamah*, or the ground. There's a symbiotic relationship between human and the earth.

At first Adam is a corpse — until God "breathed into his nostrils the breath of life" and he became something more, a "living being." In a way, we're all just dust filled up with the breath of God.

This means that human has no parallel in the universe.

Animals are pure physicality. They don't have what you and I call a "soul."[2] They eat, but they don't know how to set a table. They speak in a rudimentary language, but they don't have Shakespeare. They think, but they don't ponder the meaning of life.

Angels, on the other hand, are pure spirit. They are able to manifest physicality from time to time, but they are composed of spirit. They inhabit a world not made out of time and space.

But *adam* is a hybrid. He's made from the dust, from raw, uncut atomic matter, so he has physicality. But God breathed into his nostrils, so he has a spirit. He's an integrated, holistic being.

That means you don't *have* a body. You *are* a body. Your skeleton, nervous system, hair, skin, sex organs, mind, memory banks, smile, personality — it's all "you."

At the same time, you are *not only* your body. You are so much more than flesh and bone. In the West, we're living in the wake of the Enlightenment, when science and reason replaced the Bible and theology as the arbiter of truth. Please don't misunderstand me. I'm not down on science at all. And I don't think science and faith are at odds. Quite the opposite. There's no better way forward than to understand the world God made. But I take serious issue with scient*ism*, which is the worldview (some would call it a religion) that says, "All that is real is what you can put under a microscope in a laboratory."[3] I don't buy it. I believe there's more.

More than what's visible to the naked eye.

More than what you can measure in a Petri dish.

And more to this strange, haunting creature called human than a spinning mass of protons, neutrons, and electrons.

Here's what this has to do with sex. God said, "It's not good for the *adam* to be alone." And he made Eve from one of Adam's ribs. Don't get hung up on the rib part. Are we reading narrative? Are we reading poetry? The point is that she's made from the dust, just like Adam. She's human.

This has profound implications on Adam and Eve's sexuality. The closing line of the story is, "That is why a man leaves his father and mother and is united to his wife, and they become one flesh."[4]

The word *one* is *echad* in Hebrew — earlier I noted that when *echad* is set alongside the word *flesh*, it essentially means "fused together at the deepest levels."

Echad is when the lines blur between a man and a woman.

Echad is when you're wrapped up so close with another human being that you're not really sure who's who anymore.

Echad is when you know and are known.

Later in the Genesis story we read, "Adam knew his wife Eve, and she became pregnant."[5] To "know" is a Hebrew idiom for sex, and it's fitting. When you make love to another person, you *know* them at the deepest levels.

Something powerful happens in sex. Two humans become *echad*. They *know* each other. And this action cannot be undone. It's irreversible.

And to God, the only relationship strong enough to hold that kind of untamed, fierce power is marriage. That's the only container that can handle the nuclear force we call sex.

In traditional Jewish culture, after the couple consummated the marriage on the wedding night, the groom waved the bedsheet out the window. If the sheet was covered in blood from the woman's torn hymen, the wedding party (which was right outside the door at the feast — *awkward* ...) cheered. But if the sheet was clean, they dragged the woman out and stoned her to death.

Let's just say they took *echad* really seriously.

To clarify, I do not think we should stone men and women for sleeping together before marriage! But I do think we need to up the ante in how we think about sex.

Plato and the prostitutes

This language of *echad* is reused by Paul much later in *1 Corinthians*. He's writing to the church in Corinth about sex, and he quotes

Genesis 2. "Do you not know that your bodies are members of Christ himself? Shall I then take the members of Christ and unite them with a prostitute? Never! Do you not know that he who unites himself with a prostitute is one with her in body? For it is said [and here comes the Genesis story], 'The two will become one flesh.'"[6]

What in the world was going on in Corinth? Our church has its share of issues, but I've never had to give a sermon on why they should stop going to prostitutes.

First-century Corinth, though, is something of a legend. It was the Las Vegas of the ancient Mediterranean world.

"What happens in Corinth, stays ..."

The city was built on a thin isthmus between the Aegean and the Adriatic seas. Sailors would dock in the harbor and walk the four-and-a-half mile trek to the other side.[7] And the thousands of sailors, merchants, and travelers made Corinth a hub for prostitution.

In Paul's day, "Corinthian" was slang for a call girl. Can you imagine? "Stay away from her. She's a Portlander ..."

Plus, Corinth was near Athens, home to Plato, Aristotle, and other great Greek philosophers. Athens was the birthplace of dualism. So the idea of a "spiritual world" and a "physical world" was commonplace. I mean, Plato flat-out called the body "the prison-house" of the soul.[8] In Corinth, people were saying things like, "Food for the stomach and the stomach for food, and God will destroy them both."[9]

And this line of thinking made its way into the church. The Corinthians started thinking about sex, "Hey, it's just physical. I have a stomach, and when I get hungry, I eat. I have sex organs, and when I get horny, I have sex with prostitutes. What's the big deal? It's just biological, nothing more."

So Paul starts talking about this thing called *porneia*.[10] He writes, "The body, however, is not meant for sexual immorality but for the Lord."[11] The phrase "sexual immorality" is *porneia* in Greek, and it's a junk-drawer word. Paul means any and all forms of sexuality outside of marriage between a man and a woman. Everything from sleeping with your boyfriend or girlfriend, friends with benefits, casual sex, oral sex, adultery, and prostitution to porn, raunchy movies, adult films, strip clubs — it's all *porneia*. And it's all a cheap parody of what God created back in the garden.

Then Paul writes, "Do you not know that he who unites himself with a prostitute is one with her in body?" And then he quotes *Genesis*! "For it is said, 'The two will become one flesh.'"

He's saying, "Don't you get it? Sex is about so much more than sex. Sex is about two people becoming *one*!"

God's view of sex is actually much higher than the world's. It's easy to miss that, with all the negative rhetoric about sex in the church. But it's true. The world says sex is just biological — just the momentary coupling of two bodies for sexual release. What's the big deal? It's just recreation between consenting adults.

But God says sex is *so much more*! It's two separate, autonomous human beings fused into one. It's the melding of two bodies *and* two souls. It's physical *and* spiritual, because there's no way to bifurcate the two. That's why there's no such thing as casual sex, because sex involves *all of you.*

Couples who sleep together early in their relationship often end up dating longer than they should, even when all their friends and family are saying they're not a good match. Why? Because sex connected them at a primal level that's hard to break. What should have been a relationship that lasted a few months and then ended in a magnanimous parting of ways ends up becoming a relationship that lasts a few years and ends in heartache, pain, and regret.

You leave a piece of yourself behind with every partner you have. The more people you sleep with, the more you start to hollow yourself out until you have little or nothing left to give away.

Inside of marriage, this joining is incredible. Sex is like gravity. It keeps you in orbit with each other. Every time my wife and I make love, we're re-fused. In sync. In tune. We're *echad.*

That's why a few paragraphs later, Paul commands the married couples in Corinth to have sex regularly. Because for married couples, the best way to fight *porneia* is to make love to each other. A lot. (By the way, the Bible is seriously awesome.)

Outside of marriage, however, this melding is dehumanizing and destructive. Sex can turn men and women into objects for self-gratification. It can tear people apart. Every time you break *echad*, a part of you is lost. Some of you know the pain all too well. Is fifteen minutes of ecstasy really worth all that trauma?

I know it's hard to close the door on temptation when it's standing on the front steps. I've been there — literally. When I was dating my wife, I would get off work at 10:00 p.m. and head over to her house for an hour or so before bed, but there were nights when I had to force myself to get up and go home. The pull to sex was one click shy of irresistible, and I knew I couldn't say no if I stayed. I don't think there's any temptation harder to fight off than *porneia*. But the fact is, you can have a short period of pain followed by a lifetime of pleasure — or you can have a short period of pleasure followed by a lifetime of pain.

That's why Paul's closing exhortation is, "Flee from sexual immorality."[12] Or put another way, "Run for your life from *porneia*!" "All other sins a person commits are outside the body, but whoever sins sexually, sins against their own body."

What an interesting way to put it — "sins against their own body." When you step outside God's relational framework for sex (which is marriage), you're doing damage to *yourself*. And there is no prophylactic for the pain of sexual immorality. Nobody is immune.

Now, I don't know your story. Maybe your soul is bleeding right now. You've learned this truth the hard way. If only you could go back in time. If only you could have another chance. Then maybe, just maybe you could avoid the damage. Listen, here's the good news. Sex is powerful, but God is even more so. Do not underestimate what he can do in your life to put you back together. As a pastor, I get a front-row seat to watch the devastating effects of sin. But I also get to watch Jesus do his healing work. And I cannot tell you how many people I've seen renewed from the inside out after the tearing of *echad*.

We have a guy in our church who's coming out of a gnarly past. Drugs, alcohol, and all that goes with that. Last weekend he was sitting in worship when he looked across the room and saw a prostitute he had once hired. As you can imagine, he was torn up. After the gathering, the Spirit moved him to go to her, apologize, and make things right.

That's got Jesus written all over it.

Paul wraps up his teaching in the *1 Corinthians* passage by writing, "You are not your own; you were bought at a price. Therefore honor God with your bodies." [13]

In the first century, Corinth was a hub for sex trafficking all over the Roman Empire. There was a slave market right in the center of town. Women were bought and sold like property. But if you wanted to, you could go to the market, buy a woman, set her free, and make her your wife.

That's the imagery. Our God is the God who goes down to the slave market. He buys the shattered human who's known nothing but the pain of rape, prostitution, and shame, and he calls her his bride. And he makes her into something beautiful.

I am that woman.

Maybe you are too.

Why would we ever go back? Why would we ever cheat on that kind of a Lover?

Tree of life

I live in Portland, Oregon, which is this great city in the Pacific Northwest that's buzzing with culture. We've got art, film, design, an incredible music scene. Foodies come here on vacation just to eat — and there's no better city for coffee in the world. For obvious reasons, twentysomethings are moving to the city in droves. One comedian called it "the place where young people go to retire."[1]

Our church meets downtown by Powell's Books, a landmark independent bookstore that takes up a whole block. Because of Portland's draw to young people and a few other factors, about half of the church is under the age of thirty and single. That makes my job really fun.

And whenever I talk about sex, I get a flood of questions about "the line."

How far is too far?

What about kissing? What kind is okay? How much?

What about oral sex? Does that count?

I love it. But over the years I've figured out that what people are really asking is, "How close can I get to sin without it being sin?"

It makes me think of the story of Samson in the book of *Judges*. It has all the ingredients for a page-turner. Love, hate, sex, passion, violence, revenge, war—it's all there. The well-known part is about Samson and a Philistine feline named Delilah. Their relationship goes south in a hurry, and Samson's life ends in tragedy.

But that's not the story I mean.

I mean the story before the story.

When Samson was in his mother's womb, God put a special calling on his life. God spoke to his mother and said, "The boy is to be a Nazirite, dedicated to God from the womb. He will take the lead in delivering Israel from the hands of the Philistines."[2]

A Nazirite was a rare breed of Jew who was "dedicated to God" for a period of time, usually a year. There were three rules for a Nazirite (on top of the 613 in the Torah). First, you weren't allowed to cut your hair. Second, you weren't allowed to drink wine. And finally, you weren't allowed to touch a dead body. Ever. There's this passage in the Torah about the Nazirite vow, and it goes so far as to say that if your mother or father dies, you're not even allowed to go to the funeral.[3]

God takes this vow really seriously.

What made Samson unique is that he was a Nazirite from birth. Not for a year or two, but for life. But the first story we read about Samson is anything but Naziritish. He goes down to Timnah, which is a Philistine city on the coast, and falls in love with an unnamed woman. This isn't a great start to Samson's life. The Philistines had been oppressing Israel for years. Samson was supposed to deliver Israel from the Philistines, not flirt with their women.

But Samson starts going back and forth from his hometown in Israel and Timnah. On one of his trips he is attacked by a lion. The author of *Judges* writes, "The Spirit of the LORD came powerfully upon him so that he tore the lion apart with his bare hands as he might have torn a young goat."[4]

Because we all know how easy it is to go postal on a young goat.

Not long after the incident with the lion, he's on another trip over to Timnah, and he hears a buzzing sound off to the side of the road. It's a swarm of bees that made a hive in the lion's carcass. Now, honey in Samson's day was a rare delicacy, too good to pass up, vow or no vow. But the Torah was crystal clear. He's not allowed to touch a dead body, no matter what! But Samson inches up to the carcass, scoops out a handful of honey, being careful to avoid touching the dead animal, and goes off with honey on his lips and a smile on his face.

His toes are right on the line.

The point is that long before Samson ever fell into Delilah's trap, there were patterns in his life that set him up for disaster. That's the meaning of the lion story. It's the author's way of saying that

Samson's heart was out of sync from an early age. He was always tiptoeing right up to the line and peering over the edge.

There's a Samson in all of us, right? We have this bent to get as close to sin as we can without actually sinning. To inch up to the carcass and scoop out the honey, and then run off like nothing ever happened.

That's why, when it comes to sex, we ask questions about "the line." As followers of Jesus, we know that sex outside of marriage is wrong, but there's a whole lot of ground between a first kiss and intercourse. How far can we go?

If we don't touch the lion, can we eat the honey?

My answer is always the same. *You're asking the wrong questions.*

The kind of questions you should be asking are — "How holy can I make this? How pure? How can I shape this relationship to be special and stand out from the crowd?"

After all, who wants to settle for ordinary?

Qodesh

We don't talk much about holiness anymore. It's out of vogue.

Not that long ago, there was a global move of God we call "the holiness movement." It started with the British preacher John Wesley.

He moved over to America and toured the country on horseback. From Boston to Savannah, this guy made the rounds. They say he traveled four thousand miles a year on horseback and preached forty thousand sermons in his lifetime. Busy guy. And he had this crazy idea that the people of God should actually live like God. After all, since we have the exact same Spirit in us as Jesus, anything is possible.

Novel idea, huh?

But that was a couple hundred years ago. "Holiness" isn't even language we're used to anymore, but there's something there we need to recapture.

Let's take another look at holiness, because it has a lot to do with how we come at sex. The word *holy* is *qodesh* in Hebrew. At the heart of its meaning is the concept of "dedicated to." The root idea is "special, unique, different from the norm."

The opposite of holy isn't evil. It's ordinary, common, go with the crowd.

This word is used hundreds of times in the Hebrew Scriptures, but one phrase in particular pops up over and over again—"holy to the LORD." Interesting language, right? Holy *to* the Lord. To be holy means to be dedicated to God. Set apart for a special, unique relationship with him.

Kind of like a marriage.

In fact, the primary metaphor throughout Scripture for God's relationship to his people is that of a marriage. Yahweh, the Lord, is the husband, and Israel (and later the church) is the bride. Even the Ten Commandments are set in that motif. They're written in the language of an ancient Near Eastern wedding ceremony. At Mount Sinai, Israel is "married" to Yahweh. That's why the first commandment is, "You shall have no other gods before me."[5] It's God's way of saying, "You shall have no other lovers. I'm your husband. You're mine, and I'm yours."

That's how we need to understand holiness — as stepping into a marriage with God.

On my wedding day, the pastor asked me, "Do you take this woman to be your lawful wedded wife, to have and to hold from this day forward, for better for worse, for richer for poorer, in sickness and in health, to love and to cherish, till death do you part?" And I spoke two words that changed my life forever. "I do."

In that moment, did any of the guests think I was a killjoy because I had just turned down love with other women? Or because I had just made a promise to love her even when I didn't feel like it? Of course not. My wife is a stunning human being on so many levels. I'd like to think every single guy there was jealous. I was saying no to all sorts of freedoms, but I was saying yes to Tammy.

The same is true for holiness. We have to say no to all sorts of things, but we do so in order to say yes to life with God.

One of the best-known lines in the Old Testament is in the book of *Leviticus* ...

"Be holy, because I, the Lord your God, am holy."[6]

What a strange thing to say. You'd think God would say, "Be holy, because it's the best way to be fully awake and alive, to be fully human." After all, that's true. But to God, that's the secondary motivation. The primary motivation is to be holy, *because God is holy.*

Old Testament scholar Christopher Wright says about that passage in *Leviticus*, "All through the chapter runs the refrain: 'I am the Lord,' as if to say, '*Your* quality of life must reflect *my* character. This is what I require of *you* because this is what reflects *me*. This is what I myself would do.'"[7]

To be holy, then, is *to be like God.* That was God's intent in the beginning. We were made in God's image. We were supposed to be like God all along, but sin warped our humanness. When we live holy, we are remade into God's image. Nothing is more Godlike, and nothing is more human.

We've come a long way from John Wesley and the horse tour. If anything, we're living in a global move *away* from holiness. There's a massive overreaction to legalism in the church right now, and the pendulum is swinging with a vengeance. The word *legalistic* is fast becoming a moniker for anybody with the guts to call out sin. We're tired of being different from the norm. We want to fit in and be cool.

We want to show the world you don't have to be a social oddball to follow Jesus, and we're willing to do *anything* to prove it.

I grew up in the church, and I fully get why this is happening. Legalism is nasty stuff. Jesus spent most of his time fighting with conservatives, not liberals. The overreaction is well deserved. But I have no doubt that, in the same way many people my age grew up in "legalistic" churches, most of my children's friends are going to grow up in churches with the exact opposite problem. And trust me, it's no better.

We're Samson. And it's only a matter of time until we wake up from our nap, only to see Delilah sneaking out the back door to collect her money from the Philistines.

Joy

Somewhere along the way we forgot that God is after our joy.[8]

He's a lover, and you're the bride. He's a creator, and you're the creation. And to a greater degree than anyone else on the planet, God wants what's best for you. Especially when it comes to sex. *God wants you to have incredible sex.* The kind you dream about. The kind everybody is searching for. God wants that for you!

And God, your maker and your lover, says that kind of sex is found in marriage. Guess what? He's right. Shocking, I know. Study after study shows that the people with the best sex lives are monogamous, heterosexual married couples who had few or no partners before marriage.

Really? Yes.

And the reciprocal is true. The people who report the lowest levels of sexual satisfaction are promiscuous singles with frequent sexual encounters.[9]

Reality is 180 degrees removed from what culture tries to tell us.

When was the last time you saw a movie with a married couple in their forties having great sex on their twenty-year wedding anniversary? Or a single, thin, drop-dead gorgeous woman waking up the morning after feeling hollow and alone? But statistically, that is reality. Ask around, if you feel up to it.

Tammy and I have made love countless times, and it keeps getting better. Sure, we have ups and downs, like all lovers, but every year it's more fun.

That's what God wants for you. Joy. Nothing less. Remember, he's a God of pleasure! He created this world for you to enjoy. That's God's heart. Don't let anyone steal that joy from you. And don't you steal that joy from *anyone*, no matter how much you claim to love them.

Sibling robbery

This idea of stealing joy is found in another one of Paul's letters, *1 Thessalonians*. Quite a few scholars think it's one of the earliest writings in the entire New Testament. The church in Thessalonica was a healthy, thriving church, but just as it is for you and me, sex was a huge issue.

Paul writes, "It is God's will that you should be sanctified: that you should avoid sexual immorality."[10]

People ask me all the time, "What is God's will for my life?" Here it is. Spelled out for you in black-and-white. "Avoid *porneia*." Like the plague.

Paul doesn't stop there, however. He goes on to write, "Each of you should learn to control your own body in a way that is *holy* and honorable, not in passionate lust like the pagans, who do not know God; and that in this matter [i.e., sex] no one should wrong or *take advantage of a brother or sister*. The Lord will punish all those who commit such sins, as we told you and warned you before. For God did not call us to be impure, but *to live a holy life*."[11]

Sexuality and holiness go hand in hand. So when you sleep with your brother or sister (that's Paul's language for another Jesus follower), you "take advantage of" them. That phrase can be translated "defraud" or "steal from."

We don't think about sex as a form of theft, but it is. When you have sex with anyone other than your spouse, you're stealing from their joy. Defrauding them of what God wants for them.

"But I love her!"

I'm not sure I agree. I think you *lust* her. That's different. Love is about giving. Lust is about getting.

"But I need him!"

Are you positive? Or is it that you *want* him? That you're searching for happiness in him rather than in God?

Have you ever read the poem in *1 Corinthians*?[12] The one about how "love is patient, love is kind. It does not envy ..."? Notice, the *first* descriptor on the list is "patient." Love is not in a rush to climb under the covers. The poem goes on to say love's not "self-seeking." It wants what's best for the other, not just the instant gratification of sexual release. This is how we are to love each other.

Paul's language of "brothers and sisters" is key when it comes to sex. When Paul was writing to his young protégé, Timothy (who, as far as we know, was single), he said, "Treat ... younger women as sisters, with absolute purity."[13]

Even in *Song of Songs*, with all its erotica, the king calls the Shulammite "my sister, my bride," as if to say that she's his sister *before* she's his lover.[14]

Here's a good rule of thumb for how you treat another man or woman. *Would you be happy if somebody treated your sibling that way?* I have two younger sisters, and like most older brothers, I'm crazy-overprotective. What if we were to think of all women that way? And sisters, what if you were to do the same?

I started dating my first legit girlfriend, Emily, when I was a junior in high school. She was great. Smart as a whip, funny, with bright green eyes. And she was seventeen, a year older than me.

That's right.

I have this amazing dad. He's old-school. No tact. He doesn't beat around the bush. After Emily and I started dating, he sat me down and said, "John Mark, treat her like you would treat your sister. If you guys break up, and one day in the future you meet her husband, you should be able to look him in the eye and shake his hand without a twinge of guilt. And he should be able to say to you, 'Thank you for taking such great care of my Emily.'"

Emily and I broke up at the end of my junior year. She went on to become the valedictorian of our class and get her PhD.

I went on to ... start a band.

But I will never forget my dad's advice. As much as I hated to hear it, he was right. He was teaching me the way of Jesus.

Sin, trust, and why there will always be two trees

All this talk about holiness and joy and how you express your sexuality before marriage is actually talk about trust.

When you're dating, you're setting the stage for the rest of your life. That's why your sexuality on the way to marriage is vital. You're either building trust or tearing it down — and you will need a heaping supply of trust to make your marriage last for the long haul.

Fast-forward to your ten-year anniversary. Your husband is out of town on business. You're pregnant. You weigh fifty pounds more than you did when you were dating. And you feel insecure. If he couldn't keep his hands in his pockets when you were dating, what's to say he can now? He's on the other side of the country, the infatuation's cooled off, and you're not at your best. Can you trust him?

Or guys, imagine yourself ten years from now. It's been a long, hard decade, and you're tired. Worn down. Life has its ups and downs, but at this point, you're spent. You're not the Casanova you once were. You're working at it, but you just can't keep up the romantic magnetism. Your wife feels like your marriage is a letdown. She wants it to feel like it used to in the beginning, but you just can't re-create the past. Will she run off to another man to satisfy her desire for romance? Or will she walk with you through hardship? Can you trust her?

Sex inside of marriage opens you up to trust and vulnerability.

Remember *echad*? But in an ironic twist, sex outside of marriage works backward, and in the end, it makes it harder for you to trust another person. Because it's all the pleasure of sex minus the covenant of marriage. There's no "till death do us part," and because of that, there's little or no trust.

But this isn't just about trusting each other. This is about trusting God.

Sin, at its root, is not trusting God.

Think of Eve in the garden. Eden is full of life — plants, animals, and rampant beauty. In the middle of all that, there are two trees — the tree of life and the tree of the knowledge of good and evil. God is crystal clear. "You are free to eat from any tree in the garden; but you must not eat from the tree of the knowledge of good and evil, for when you eat from it *you will certainly die.*"[15]

But then Eve sees the fruit hanging there on the tree. So delicious. So tempting. And the serpent whispers in her ear, "You will not certainly die. For God knows that when you eat from it your eyes will be opened, and you will be like God, knowing good and evil."[16]

What he's really saying is, "God's not good. He doesn't care about your joy. He's mean and fickle. You know better than God. Go ahead. Do what *you* feel is right."

And who does Eve trust? The serpent. She thought he knew the path to joy better than God. And she was wrong. Not only that, but she missed out on life! To me, that's the crazy part. There were *two* trees in the middle of Eden. The tree of life was a one-way ticket to live forever. But she missed out, all because of misplaced trust.

We want to make not sinning about self-control. In the moment of temptation, we clamp down our jaw, make a fist, and say no. And that's fine. But really it's about faith more than anything. It's about giving up control, and trusting God.

Who do you believe? The serpent or God? What do you trust? Your own moral compass or God's wisdom?

The serpent says the best sex is found in short, risky, promiscuous relationships with beautiful people. God says the best sex is found when a man and a woman say, "Till death do us part."

It's all about who you trust.

Do you trust that the way of Jesus is the best way to live?

Do you trust that what looks like freedom is actually slavery, and "repressing" your sexual desire may just be the best thing to ever happen to you?

Do you trust that God's heart for you is good? That God's heart for you is joy?

Because if you do, there's a tree of life in the middle of the garden, and you're invited to come and eat.

Part 4

Romance

The Song

God is a romantic.

The closing image in the Scriptures is of the marriage of heaven and earth. The prophet John sees the city of God "prepared as a bride beautifully dressed for her husband."[1] From the beginning of the Bible all the way to the last page, it's like God just can't get enough of *ahava*.

We're no different. Why would we be when we're made in God's likeness? Romance is embedded into our DNA. We're born with a missing rib, with a sixth sense that someone is out there, waiting. It makes perfect sense that we would grow up dreaming about that someone, that day.

One of my favorite cities in the world is London, England. Maybe it's because my wife and I started our life together on its streets. That does something to the psyche. I love Westminster Abbey. Parts of the cathedral are more than a thousand years old. People have been praying, learning, worshiping, doubting, and experiencing God there for more than a millennium. The Abbey is also where all the British Royals tie the knot. The wedding of the decade — Prince William to Kate Middleton — happened there, and more than a billion people tuned in to watch the ceremony. That's one out of every seven humans on the planet. I know a few people in my city who woke up at 4:00 a.m. to watch the ceremony live. Why?

Maybe it's idealism. Maybe it's that we were raised on a steady diet of propaganda from Hollywood. Or maybe it's a dormant gene, something deep inside us, that scientists have yet to unearth. Maybe it's all of the above.

But what's shocking to me is that when we actually get into a relationship and the fantasy becomes a reality, so often we're clueless about how to go forward. We're inundated with culture's dogmatic vision of what a relationship should (and shouldn't) look like, but we know it's a warped picture. The problem is, we just don't have a better one. It's like we're flying blind.

In short, we don't know what loveology looks like.

We don't know what romantic relationships should look like when seen through God's eyes. It's a long walk from "hello" to "I do," and we don't have a picture, a paradigm, a frame of reference to show the way.

That's where *The Song* comes in.

For a long time, this obscure, evocative poetry book has been buried under layers of allegory and hyperspiritualization. Like I said before, I know some people read it as an allegory about God and his people, and that's fine, but I just can't get there.

In scholarship there's a whole branch of theology called hermeneutics, which is the art and science of how to interpret the Scriptures. One of the first things you learn is called "authorial intent." You're always asking the question, "What was the original author trying to say? What's his message? What's his point?"

When you read *Song of Songs* with that lens, I just don't see how you can read it as anything less than God's celebration of romantic love. The author is in love with love, and he thinks God is too. But we're scared to read the text at face value. Can it really be that God is *that* into romantic love? I think the answer is yes. Absolutely.

Now, most of the book is about sex, but a good deal of it is about the relationship between a king and his lover, a working-class shepherdess called the Shulammite. It's not easy to interpret — after all, it's poetry. But there are themes that pop up all the way through that can help us to date well. Glimpses of what a healthy relationship looks like. The kind of relationship that God puts his stamp of approval on and says, "Yes, well done. Write that down. Put *that* in the Scriptures." It's the picture, the paradigm, we need to construct a relationship that will carry us to our wedding day with joy.

In *The Song* we find four marks of a healthy relationship. By "relationship" I mean love, romance, and sexuality *before* marriage. Maybe you call that dating, or maybe you kissed dating good-bye and call it something else, or maybe you're from the East and your parents decide who you marry. Whatever the case, here are four marks of what your relationship should look like on the way to marriage.

We'll talk about *the line*, *the friends*, and *the journey to the day*, but first we begin with ...

The chase

At the beginning of the poem, we read about the king inviting the Shulammite on a date. It's written in the woman's voice, which makes it all the more interesting ...

> Listen! My beloved!
>   Look! Here he comes,
> leaping across the mountains,
>   bounding over the hills.
> My beloved is like a gazelle or a young stag.
>   Look! There he stands behind our wall,
> gazing through the windows,
>   peering through the lattice.
> My beloved spoke and said to me,
>   "Arise, my darling,
>   my beautiful one, come with me.
> See! The winter is past;
>   the rains are over and gone.
> Flowers appear on the earth;
>   the season of singing has come,
> the cooing of doves
>   is heard in our land.

The fig tree forms its early fruit;
    the blossoming vines spread their fragrance.
Arise, come, my darling;
    my beautiful one, come with me."[2]

Spring. For thousands of years, more than any other season, spring has been the symbol of love. It's the time when new life is starting to bud, sprout, and grow. Color is breaking through the ground. The sun is thawing out the frozen earth. And *ahava* is doing the exact same thing. It's in the air. It's viral and contagious.

The opening story of springtime love is a vivid picture of the king calling his love. He comes to her home, like the "young stag" he is, and the first words on his lips are, "Arise, my darling, my beautiful one, come with me." In fact, he says it *twice*, at the beginning and end of the poem. He's wooing this woman. Calling her to come away.

That's the man's job. To chase, to pursue, to draw the woman into a relationship. In the next stanza he says …

My dove in the clefts of the rock,
    in the hiding places on the mountainside,
show me your face,
    let me hear your voice;
for your voice is sweet,
    and your face is lovely.

He's coaxing her out of hiding. Creating a safe place for her. Calling her into the open.

You're beautiful.

And I'm *after you.*

But it's not like the Shulammite is passive in the chase. She's anything but shy. In the opening stanza of the book she says, "Take me away with you — let us hurry!" She *wants* the man to take her away, to chase after her. She lets the king know she's waiting, and she wants him to knock on her door.

That's how God intended male-female relationships to thrive. It's a two-way street, for sure, but it's the man's job to instigate and activate, to lead the way.

Why? Because from Genesis 2 on, men are called to *lead.* It's Adam who is first on the ground in Eden. It's Adam who sings over his wife. It's Adam who calls her "woman." It's the man who will leave his father and mother — not the woman.

In the New Testament, Paul makes a comment about how "Adam was formed first, then Eve."[3] All he means by that is men carry a responsibility to lead. By "lead" I *do not* mean boss around, take charge, dominate, intimidate, or any other stupid thing that men have done in the name of the the Bible. I mean step out, take responsibility, care for, listen to, love, *serve* ... and risk.

And that is scary. Because every time you step out, there's a chance you'll fall through the ice. You risk failure and rejection. You know that feeling when you finally get up the nerve to ask a girl out — and she says *no*? It's horrible. The pain of rejection is deafening. But *rejection is a part of life*. No matter how hard you try to insulate yourself, at some point you will fail. It's only a matter of time.

And a vital part of becoming a man or a woman is learning to take risks. Learning to fail, and to fail well. That's true for love, but it's also true for education, your career, the gospel — all of life. If we aren't willing to take risks, we will never grow beyond an impoverished version of ourselves. Of who we could have been.

If you want to learn to ride a bike, you have to take off the training wheels. And that means you are going to crash and burn. It's gonna happen. *But it's worth it.*

I have two boys, Jude and Moses. The mantra of modern-day parenting can be summed up in two words — "Be careful!" Go to a park and listen to the chatter for five minutes. You will hear that phrase dozens of times.

I work really hard to never say that to my boys. I prefer the phrase, "You can do it! It's not that high — go for it!" Maybe that's irresponsible on my part. It's just that I'm not scared of Jude falling out of a tree and breaking his arm, but I am *terrified* of Jude growing up to be the kind of man who won't climb a tree. This is true for both boys *and* girls. I also have a daughter, Sunday, and I want her to grow up with a fierce courage to dream and dare to follow God's call on her life. But this is especially true of boys.

One of the most disheartening traits in a man is cowardice.

As followers of Jesus — male and female — we are called to live by faith. That means we can risk. We live in a world where the tomb is empty and anything is possible.

The gospel gives us the freedom to fail. Because *we are loved*. No matter what happens. Whether we succeed or not. Whether the business venture works out or not. Whether we get into that school or have to settle for second best. Whether she says yes or he doesn't return your call. It doesn't matter. Our self-worth doesn't come from any of that. Which means we are free to risk, to fail, and to get back up and try again. It's okay.

Love is a chase. A dance between a man and a woman. And it starts when a man says, "Come away," and the woman says, "Let us hurry ..."

The line

Just because the Shulammite is a "sealed fountain"[4] (or a virgin) on her wedding night doesn't mean she isn't sexualized. Before her wedding, she's charged with sexual desire for her lover. "Take me away with you — let us hurry! Let the king bring me into his chambers."[5] And after her wedding, she is, by far, the more sexual of the two.[6]

All throughout *Song of Songs* there's this refrain, this chorus, that the Shulammite keeps coming back to ...

> His left arm is under my head,
>   and his right arm embraces me.
> Daughters of Jerusalem, I charge you
>   by the gazelles and by the does of the field:
> Do not arouse or awaken love
>   until it so desires.[7]

The beginning of this refrain is about foreplay. "His left arm is under my head, and his right arm ..." She's deeply enjoying sex with her husband. But the second part is a word to her unmarried friends, the "daughters of Jerusalem." It's a warning of sorts — not to "arouse or awaken love until it so desires," until the right time, until there's a context in which to play out these desires.

We're back to the question about "the line." We're sexual beings — and that's good. God made us that way. And he made marriage as the context for us to enjoy sex. There's no better place. But we're sexualized long before our wedding night. So how do we express our sexuality *on the way* to marriage? What's okay? What's off limits?

To the Shulammite, the question isn't "how far can we go?" but "when can we start?"

Her advice is simple and worth following. *Don't wake up the sexual part of your relationship until you can follow it all the way through.* That means don't go anywhere near the line until your wedding day.

She says this not once, not twice, but *three times.* At the beginning, middle, and end of the poem. In ancient literature like the Bible, whenever a phrase is repeated, it's for emphasis. It's her way of driving home the point—"Listen! You need to get this!"

Nothing does more to sabotage a relationship than *porneia.* It's lethal. Here are three reasons. There are more, but let's just start with three.

The first one we already covered. In sex, two become *echad,* or one. You are joined together. Inside of marriage this is a life-giving thing, but outside, that kind of unbridled, fierce power is explosive. Two people become one, long before any covenant is made. A relationship that should last a few weeks instead lasts a few years, and a story that should end with a gracious parting of ways ends in regret and remorse. It happens all the time.

Secondly, sex obscures your vision. Judgment goes out the window. We've all seen the girl dating the guy (or the other way around) who's a jerk, and all her friends are saying, "Are you crazy? You can do so much better. Don't waste your life on him! You should break up." But for some odd reason, she can't see it. Nine times out of ten she's sleeping with him. And any objectivity she once had is long gone. It's obvious they're not a good fit, but she's blind to it.

When you have sex, you're not able to accurately "see" the person you're dating. Once again, in marriage, this is beautiful! "Love covers over a multitude of sins,"[8] and sex sure helps. But outside of marriage, this just makes a bad problem worse.

Third, even if you end up marrying the person you're fooling around with, you can't build a relationship on sex. You just can't. For starters, it's not sustainable. At some point you want more out of a relationship than foreplay. You want a friend. A partner. A mother or father for your children. You want to do life together. You want to enjoy each other's company long after your ability to make love has faded. But when you're dating, there's no way to know if you have that kind of chemistry until you spend a season of life together where sex is not involved.

For all those reasons, and more, the Shulammite's refrain is invaluable. Listen to her. Listen to *God.* Don't arouse or awaken the sexual part of your relationship until your wedding night. When that night comes, you'll discover it was more than worth the wait.

The friends

The Song is really more like a play than a song. It has characters — the king, the Shulammite, and this mysterious group we don't know much about, the "friends." These are other people who speak into the relationship. They have a voice.

From the beginning, the friends affirm the relationship as a good thing. The first thing they say is …

We rejoice and delight in you;
>> we will praise your love more than wine.[9]

They think well of the king. He's a good man. The Shulammite is on the right track.

Later they help the couple navigate the road to marriage. At one point the Shulammite doesn't know the king's whereabouts. They say ...

If you do not know, most beautiful of women,
>> follow the tracks of the sheep
and graze your young goats
>> by the tents of the shepherds.[10]

And when the couple is in conflict, they help the Shulammite see the good in her lover ...

How is your beloved better than others,
>> most beautiful of women?
How is your beloved better than others,
>> that you so charge us?[11]

They call her to think about what she loves in her husband and to focus on that. To call out the good in him rather than criticize the bad.

The point is that *this couple wasn't alone*. A story about a king and a shepherd girl is also a story about her friends and parents and family and village. And they all had a voice with which to give input. Wisdom. Rebuke. Clarification.

We live in what is, hands down, the most hyperindividualistic society in the world, but there is no way to date well in isolation. You have to be a part of a community.

For the first time in human history, dating is usually disconnected from family and friends. How often do you see a couple get together and then go into hibernation? All of a sudden they are MIA. Next thing you know, you're getting asked to be a groomsman or brides-maid at a wedding for somebody you haven't even seen in a year!

It doesn't have to be that way. Orthodox Jews have a practice of matchmaking called the *shidduch*. Friends and family suggest potential partners for single men and women, and then they meet to get to know each other. The couple usually has the final say, but nothing gets the ball rolling like a good old-fashioned *shidduch*.

To clarify, I'm not saying you need to start a *shidduch* at your church. (Although I'm sure your parents would love the idea.) I'm just saying that if you open up your relationship to people you know and trust and give them a voice to speak into your relationship, it will do well.

That will mean, however, that you open up your relationship to scru-tiny. You can't hide. You have to be honest with people about the good and the bad. As a result, though, they will help you think straight. Help you make wise decisions, sidestep mistakes, and walk at the right pace.

Who are your "friends"? Your community? Who are the people you know and trust? Are you inviting them to speak into your relationship? And are you listening?

The journey to the day

At the crux of the king's poem, the story finally turns the corner to marriage. We read about the long-awaited wedding day ...

> Who is this coming up from the wilderness
>   like a column of smoke,
> perfumed with myrrh and incense
>   made from all the spices of the merchant?
> Look! It is Solomon's carriage,
>   escorted by sixty warriors,
>   the noblest of Israel ...
> Daughters of Jerusalem, come out,
>   and look, you daughters of Zion.
> Look on King Solomon wearing a crown,
>   the crown with which his mother crowned him
> on the day of his wedding,
>   the day his heart rejoiced.[12]

The first half of *The Song* has a tension to it. A movement, if you will. The king is "coming up" from the desert, from solitude, to the wedding and to his bride.

The poetry builds and escalates and crescendos to the wedding day.

That's what a healthy relationship is like. It has motion, inertia, cartography. There's a beginning and an end to the journey. It's *going somewhere.*

All healthy relationships are either moving toward or away from marriage. That's a key piece of romance before marriage. To answer the question, "Should we spend our life together?"

Dating to date is stupid. It's a waste of your heart, and it's a waste of time. You're not looking for a boyfriend or girlfriend. You're looking for a husband or wife.

Now, I don't think this means you need to stress out over a relationship, like you have to "know" right away. If anything, I think most couples take dating way too seriously. Relax. It's a cup of coffee.

But I do think this means you shouldn't date until you're ready, or at least close to ready, to get married. At least not seriously. I'm not saying it's a sin to date if your mom's still driving you to school every day. But if you're twelve, you have to ask, "Where is this relationship going?"

There's a brilliant one-liner in *Proverbs.* "Put your outdoor work in order and get your fields ready; after that, build your house."[13]

So good.

Your "fields" in the ancient Near East was your job, your source of income. Your "house" was your family. The voice of wisdom says,

"First get your life in order and then start down the road to marriage and family."

That does *not* mean you have to be thirty, make $100k a year, and own a home before you go on a first date. My wife and I married young and poor, which comes with pros and cons. When she said, "For richer for poorer," I said, "Definitely for poorer." But we both knew what we were called to do. Neither of us were "there" yet, but we were on the way. And we were happy to make the journey together.

The point of the proverb is that before you build your house, there's stuff you need to get done. Set in order. I think ideally you should have the trajectory set for your life. At least as much as you can know on the front end.

Because the point of your relationship *isn't your relationship*! Remember what marriage is for? Friendship, *gardening*, etc. A healthy marriage is built around a calling. And a healthy relationship gets that from the start, long before the wedding day. Every cup of coffee, every night out, every conversation, is movement, further away from or closer to "husband and wife."

Jesus has this great analogy in *The Gospel of Matthew* about building your house on a rock versus on the sand.[14] The house is a metaphor for your life as a whole, but a first-century Jew would have understood "house" as a way of saying "your family." And just as it takes time to build a house, it takes time to build a life together with your spouse.

The key line is, "Everyone who hears these words of mine and puts them into practice is like a wise man who built his house on the rock ... but everyone who hears these words of mine and does not put them into practice is like a foolish man who built his house on sand."

Jesus is saying that if you build your life on obedience to his teachings, then no matter what comes against you — rain and rising streams — your life will stand the test. But if you don't, if you go your own way, then in that moment of crisis, your life will fall to pieces.

This analogy is at the end of Jesus' Sermon on the Mount, which is Matthew's collection of Jesus' central teachings. The sermon's closing line is, "The rain came down, the streams rose, and the winds blew and beat against that house, and it fell with a great crash."

Haunting way to end a sermon, isn't it?

Jesus' analogy is essential. In the early months and years of a relationship, you're laying the foundation for your "house." This time is crucial because you're setting the stage for the rest of your life together. If you go about it the wrong way, you're a disaster waiting to happen. But if you build on Jesus' way, on obedience to his set of teachings, then your relationship will flourish, not for a month or a year, but for a lifetime.

Dig deep. Dig well.

Isaac and Rebekah

It wasn't that long ago that your parents would have made the call on who you married.

For thousands of years, marriage was arranged by your mother or father. Because marriage wasn't just about you. Are you kidding me? How narcissistic.

Marriage was about your family.

Marriage was about your clan, your tribe, *your people*.

Marriage was about so much more than a couple's feelings.

This is how it was, all over the world. In early Jewish culture, you didn't meet your wife until your wedding day. In other cultures, you had a say, or at least a voice, in who you married. But either way, your spouse was picked out for you. Who you married was considered way too important a decision to leave up to a couple of amorous, emotionally incontinent lovers.

We've come a long way over the years, thank God. But you should know that "dating" is a relative newcomer on the scene. Now, I'm a bit of a history nerd—forgive me—but this won't take long. I think it's worth knowing where dating comes from.

It wasn't until the nineteenth century that culture made the shift to "calling." The *woman* usually started the process. She would let a man know she was interested, and then he would get permission from her father and come calling on her. The couple would spend time in the woman's home—in the parlor or on the front porch. Nothing was done in secret. The relationship was on display. Public. Out in the open. The family was still involved, but it gave more freedom to the man and woman to pick and choose.

Early in the twentieth century, people started "dating." Early on, the word *date* was used as slang for getting a prostitute, but over time it lost that meaning. Dating started with the urban poor. As the West urbanized, there were no parlors or front porches, so the couple would go out on the town.

With the birth of the entertainment culture, dating spread up the socioeconomic ladder and into the culture at large. At this point romance became disconnected from the family. The family may or may not be involved, but the relationship is now closed off, private. It happens at a restaurant, in a coffee shop, at a show, or in a bedroom.[1]

I think we're actually past dating to a new form of romance. Now couples start with sex. What used to come at the *end* of a romantic relationship, as the sought-after prize once a couple crossed the finish line into marriage, now comes at the *beginning* of a relationship. A man and woman meet—at a party or bar or nightclub, at work, on a trip—and they sleep together. Instant gratification. Then if they feel like they're a fit and want to start a relationship, fine. If not, they move on.

I'm not sure if there's a name for this, other than screwed up.

Now, the Scriptures say *nothing* about dating. Dating is less than a hundred years old. The Scriptures were written thousands of years ago, in a different language, on a different continent, to a different culture. The Scriptures don't tell you how to date or court, or whatever your style is. Every form of romance has pros and cons, and any attempt to claim one as "biblical" is doomed to failure. If you want to argue for what's in the Bible, technically it's arranged marriage, and aside from a few overprotective parents, I don't think anybody wants to go back to *that*.

(Although one study of American and Indian marriages found that, on average, by the ten-year anniversary, couples with arranged marriages were far happier than couples who married for love. Interesting.)[2]

My point is that we have freedom in how we go about the journey from "hello" to "husband and wife," but that freedom needs to be shaped by what the Scriptures tell us about loveology. And even if the Bible doesn't have any advice on dating, it is filled with love stories.

One of my favorites is the story of Isaac and Rebekah. In the book of *Genesis*, God makes this staggering promise to Abraham: he's going to become a great nation that spreads God's blessing out over all the earth. And after *decades* of arduous waiting, Abraham and Sarah have a son, Isaac.

Toward the end of Abraham's life, Isaac is still single. This is a serious problem. Abraham needs to become a nation, and right now he's a widower with one son.

It's almost like marriage is about so much more than marriage ...

So Abraham sends his servant to find a wife for Isaac. (Now, that's the way to roll. Have your wealthy dad hire a guy to find you a spouse. You should think about that—it's biblical.) Abraham wants Isaac's wife to come from his tribe, so his servant heads off on a trek of a thousand miles from Israel to modern-day Iraq in search of a bride for Isaac.

When he gets to Nahor (Abraham's hometown), he stops outside the city to pray. "Lord, God of my master Abraham, make me successful today, and show kindness to my master Abraham. See, I am standing beside this spring, and the daughters of the townspeople are coming out to draw water. May it be that when I say to a young woman, 'Please let down your jar that I may have a drink,' and she says, 'Drink, and I'll water your camels too'—let her be the one you have chosen for your servant Isaac. By this I will know that you have shown kindness to my master."[3]

As far as we know, this is the first prayer in all of the Scriptures asking God for guidance. And what's it for? The right match for a marriage.

I can't think of a better thing to pray about. After the decision to follow Jesus, I would argue the most important decision you will make is who you marry. That decision will shape your life. Your children, family, where you live or don't live, what you succeed at and fail at, *your future*—all of these things hinge on who you marry. A bad decision can cripple you for life. And a good one can unleash a whole new world. A lot's at stake.

That's why the servant prays! He knows that God's on the hunt for Isaac's wife, and his job is just to figure out the who. So he goes to the well. In the ancient Near East, the well was *the spot* to find a wife. Quite a few of the love stories in the Bible actually start at a well: Moses and Zipporah, Isaac and Rebekah, Jacob and Rachel.[4]

There must be something in the water.

And God answers the servant's prayer. The text reads, "*Before he had finished praying*, Rebekah came out with her jar on her shoulder. She was the daughter of Bethuel son of Milkah, who was the wife of Abraham's brother Nahor. She was very beautiful, a virgin; no man had ever slept with her."

The servant runs up to her and asks for a drink of water. And then, in this epic moment, she says, "I'll draw water for your camels too, until they have had enough to drink."

Can you imagine how that would have sounded to the servant? *I'll draw water for your camels too ...*

Seconds after his prayer! And this was not a small thing to pray for. Camels drink about twenty-five gallons of water at a time, and there were ten camels! But Rebekah is up for the job.

I love this story because it has God's fingerprints all over it. Now, I made it clear before that I think the idea of "the one" is a myth, and a dangerous one at that. There's no "soul mate" out there who will "complete you." I honestly believe my wife and I could have married any number of people and had a chance for a happy life, as long as our marriage was rooted in a love for one another and for God and formed around God's kingdom.

But ...

I also believe that God is a romantic. And we need to nuance this out a bit. There is no doubt in my mind that God brought Tammy and me together. Our story was scripted. And I don't think we're the outlier. I believe God's *involved* in your life to the degree that you open up your story to his authorship. In the beginning God brought Eve to Adam, and I think he's been doing that ever since.

I very much believe that God can and *will* lead you to your future spouse. And if you follow Jesus, I believe that God is shaping you for that day, just like I believe God is shaping me now for things that are twenty years in my future and nowhere on my radar. God's like that. He's *involved.*

God is the original *yenta.*

Later in the story, Rebekah's parents hear the story of the servant's prayer and say, "This is from the LORD; we can say nothing to you one way or the other."[5] It was obvious. Staring everybody in the face. This was God's doing.

That's what you want before you take the plunge into marriage. A crystal-clear sense that "this is from the LORD." That God orchestrated this relationship from the start. He was at the well.

Your job is to figure out if the person you're dating is God's pick for you. Not "the one" or the mythic "missing half" from Zeus, but your Rebekah. The man or woman with whom God wants you to share the next fifty years of your life.

But this is easier said than done, because *nobody* is a perfect match. Tim Keller makes this great point about how every other person on the planet is a *bad match* for you. You're all incompatible. Nobody is a good fit. It's just that some people are a worse fit than others.[6]

And we live in this tension. On one hand, God brought Eve to Adam and put Rebekah at the well for Isaac. But on the other hand, Eve made some really bad dietary choices that cost Adam his life. Rebekah helped her son Jacob lie to Isaac and steal Esau's blessing. In fact, it was her idea. That's the world we live in. If you open up your life to God's hand, he will be involved, but *no matter who you marry*, there will be drama. It's a tension, and a lot of people err on one of two sides.

Side one …

Some people settle.

Maybe it's impatience. You're in a rush to get married. You're lonely or bored or you want sex, and you just don't want to wait anymore.

Perhaps it's fear. You're scared of growing old alone. What if you don't get another chance at this? What if he's the best you can do?

Or it could be insecurity. You don't believe you're good enough. You don't deserve the kind of woman or man you dream about. Your past, your failures, the baggage you carry — it's too much. You found somebody who will take you as is, and that's enough.

Or it could be weak faith. You don't actually trust that God is involved in your life and that his way is how you were made to live.

Whatever the reason may be, *don't settle*. It is far better to be single and unhappy than married and unhappy. The former you can change, but marriage is for life.

For some people, marriage is nothing more than a daily reminder of what could have been but isn't. It's a daily letdown. You don't want that.

If you feel pressure to get married, and to get married fast, don't capitulate. Don't cave. You know what I'm talking about. Your family, your friends, are hounding you. "When are you gonna get married?"

And it's not all bad, but the idea that you *have* to get married and you need to do so by twenty-five in order to live a meaningful life is flat-out untrue. You don't *have* to get married. Ever. And you can live an amazing life, with or without a spouse. There's more to life than marriage.

And don't marry someone you hope will change. This happens all the time. Some people change, but most don't. And people who do change, change slowly. Love, by definition, takes people the way they are, not the way you want them to be. Nobody wants to feel like a project. It's not fair to you, and it's definitely not fair to your spouse. If you don't love them right now, just as they are, then don't get married. Of course it's okay to see someone's future and believe in that, even to help them get there. But *they* have to drive it, not you. You can't take people places they don't want to go. Don't marry a project. Marry a partner.

And don't explain away the red flags. When your family and friends say stuff you don't want to hear — *listen*. Love is blind. You need to listen to people who can see. What you think is "quirky" when you've been dating for six months you'll think is flat-out annoying when you've been married for ten. Whatever you're frustrated with now in your potential spouse, ratchet it up by ten and you'll get a sense of how you'll feel down the road.

And don't forget you're not just marrying a husband or wife. You're marrying a father or mother. If you have children, your spouse's strengths and weaknesses will be passed on to your kids. You're not just giving your future to this marriage. You're giving your children's future as well.

So much is at stake. Don't give up the search. The right spouse is worth the wait.

Side two ...

Now, other people have the exact opposite problem. They set the bar so high that nobody ever makes the cut.

You know people with "the list"? You know what I'm talking about. He needs to be six foot four, black hair, green eyes, scruff but no beard, well dressed but not self-obsessed, educated but not snobby, easygoing but driven, wealthy but not greedy, romantic but not controlling — and the list is like three feet long. These people treat dating like shopping. They walk into a room and start scanning for someone who fits the profile.

One of two things happens to these people. Either they never get married, or worse, they do get married, and the marriage is a disaster. Because *nobody is ever good enough*.

This is kind of how I'm wired. There was no "list" before our marriage, but my Myers-Briggs test comes out with a one-sentence summary of my personality. "Everything has room for improvement."[7] So true. *Everything* has room for improvement. And that means everyone as well. I carry this picky, meticulous mind-set into my marriage and it does nothing but harm. My wife is incredible. Pretty, strong, wise, happy, she puts up with my flaws (which are many). And she's a joy to be around—but she's not heaven on earth.

No matter who you marry, they will have problems and issues, and, at some level, they will be a "bad match" for you. It's inevitable.

And this is exacerbated by the culture we live in. We live in a culture of options. Portland is one of the top cities in America for food and drink. You could literally go out every night for years and never make it to all the spots.

Every Thursday I take my wife on a date. We look forward to it all week. The hardest part of every Thursday is deciding where to go because there are so many options. And then when we get to a restaurant, they hand us a menu with *more* options. Sometimes after I finally make the string of decisions, I'll be sitting at the restaurant eating my meal and feeling like I might have made the wrong call.

We live with this nagging feeling that we could do better.

And this sucks the joy right out of life. As a general rule, the more options you have, the less you enjoy your choices. Rather than enjoying what is real, we fantasize about what *could be*.

It's impossible to be content if you're always wondering if there's a better option.

It's impossible to enjoy your job if you're constantly skimming the web for job openings or toying with the idea of another career.

It's impossible to put down roots in your city if you're constantly envisioning yourself in New York or Austin or Silver Lake.[8]

And it's impossible to enjoy your marriage if you're constantly thinking, "What if she was calmer? What if he was more interesting? What if she was kinder? What if he wasn't so stressed out about his job?"

What you're really thinking is, "What if I could do better?" Here's the problem—the answer to that question will always be yes. In theory. But in real life, on this small planet called earth, it's messy. When it comes to marriage, there's no perfect match. There's no "other half" floating out there in the universe that will make you "complete."

At some point you have to make a decision. Don't settle, and don't set the bar so high that you're living in a fantasy, not on terra firma. But when that day comes, and the pastor or judge or random guy-you-know-with-Internet-access says "husband and wife," then *you savor every day.*

The closing paragraph in the Isaac and Rebekah story takes place back in Canaan. Isaac "went out to the field one evening to meditate," and on the horizon, he sees the servant, the ten camels ... and Rebekah. She's finally come, after years of waiting. The text reads, "Isaac brought her into the tent of his mother Sarah, and he married Rebekah. So she became his wife, and he loved her."[9]

Orthodox Jews love to point out the sequence of the last sentence. "She became his wife, *and he loved her.*" In that order. This marriage was arranged—by Abraham and by God. The love story started *after* the wedding day.

There's a saying about marriage that Jews in the East say to Christians in the West. "We put cold soup on the fire, and it becomes slowly warm; you put hot soup into a cold plate, and it becomes slowly cold."[10]

I'm not sure if I buy that or not, but here's what I know is true: God was at the well long before Isaac and Rebekah. And before you ever get to your well, God's there ahead of you. He's involved. Your job is to meditate in the field. To draw water for the camels. To make a wise decision when the time comes, and then to enjoy every day you get.

A form of torture called waiting

1942. America is at war in Europe and in the Pacific. Millions of young men are dropping everything to go and fight. My grandfather, Bill Comer, is a senior in high school when he meets a girl named Ruth from the nearby town of Muncie, Indiana. A few months later, right after graduation, he joins the Air Force, but while he's away at basic training, they start writing letters.

They fall in love.

One
letter
at
a
time.

Ten months later she takes the train down to Alabama, where he's in training, and they get married. *Three days later* he ships out for Guam. Not exactly an ideal way to start off a marriage. He's a bomber pilot flying sorties over Japan, and she's all alone at an Air Force base in the States.

They were nineteen and twenty.

Here's what was crazy—that was normal! Most of that generation married right out of high school. But today, most of you will spend a *decade* between graduation and marriage. Tammy and I married young, but that's so rare now that it's weird. When I drop Jude off at school, I'm at least a decade younger than all the other parents. The median age for marriage in the United States is 26.5 for women and 28.7 for men.[1] And that's for those of you who actually get married. For the first time in US history, there are more single people than married people. Fewer and fewer people are getting married at all.

We've elongated the time lapse between adolescence and adulthood, and in doing so we've made the waiting period longer than ever before. You may think that's a good thing or a bad thing, but either way, waiting is a part of life. Even if you marry young, like I did, you still end up waiting. There's always something on the horizon, just out of your reach. Graduation, a job, an experience, a dream you're working toward — the list is endless.

The trick is to learn how to wait well.

Psalm 37

King David was no stranger to waiting. He spent thirteen years between his anointing as king and his coronation. That's brutal. When God has put something in you and you know it's from the Spirit and it's bursting to get out, *but ... nothing ... happens*. It's torture. Waterboarding on the soul.

David spent most of that time on the run as a fugitive from his jealous rival, King Saul. He spent years hiding under rocks in the desert.

Waiting.

Psalm 37 was probably written during that time. At En Gedi or in some alcove tucked into a mountain. It's a raw, unfiltered poem, one that questions if God's ever going to come through. And if so, when? *How much longer?*

The psalm reads ...

> Do not fret because of those who are evil
> > or be envious of those who do wrong;
> for like the grass they will soon wither,
> > like green plants they will soon die away.
> Trust in the LORD and do good;
> > dwell in the land and enjoy safe pasture.
> Take delight in the LORD,
> > and he will give you the desires of your heart.
> Commit your way to the LORD;
> > trust in him and he will do this:
> He will make your righteous reward shine like the dawn,
> > your vindication like the noonday sun.

For thousands of years, people like you and me have found solace in David's lyrics. Because David's story is our story. His lament is our lament. We all know what it feels like to be stuck waiting when we feel like we're ready to move on. When "those who are evil" thrive and flourish and get ahead, and we shrivel up on the inside and fall behind and scrape by.

How is it that people who don't follow God's way sometimes do well? Really well. How is it that those of us who *do* follow God sometimes limp along. How is that fair?

Or put another way, how is it that people who ignore loveology meet somebody, have great sex (whenever they want), get married, and do well? And how is it that thousands of Jesus followers work and fight and pray to do life God's way, but end up alone?

The truth is that God's wisdom on love and marriage and sex and romance and the rest works *as a general rule* — not as a "promise from God" in every scenario, all the time, but as wisdom. As a general rule, people who follow the way of Jesus thrive, and people who buy into culture's way don't. *But there are exceptions all over the place.* And it's the exceptions that get under our skin — that make us question why we should go through all this trouble if people who take the easy route sometimes do just fine.

David's answer is, "Just wait" … "Like the grass they will soon wither, like green plants they will soon die away." It's only a matter of time until the bottom falls out. A relationship that was built on the sand *will* fall. It might take a year or a decade or longer, but it will fall. Of course, that's not God's heart — he's all about healing and re-creation. The second you turn over your life to God, he's right there, waiting to reset the foundation in your cracked relationship, because if you don't get the foundation right, you're in for disaster.

Growing up, there was this high-end home around the corner from where I lived. It was eye-popping. Three stories. All custom. And it was built on this steep incline with a panoramic view of the city. My house had a panoramic view of ... another house.

It rains in Portland. A lot. And one spring we had a storm that lasted for weeks. I swear I saw Noah at one point. Water was everywhere. In that storm, this house literally slid right off its foundation and down the hill into a ravine. The entire house was demolished. Nobody was hurt, thank God, but there was a nasty legal battle between the homeowners and the builder. Turns out, the builder cut corners on the foundation, and it wasn't strong enough to survive the storm.

It's almost like Jesus was right.

The way of Jesus is *so* different from the world. The stuff we've been talking about in this book may as well have been written in Arabic, because it sounds like a foreign language. And Jesus' way is good, but it's hard. Really hard at times. Every cell in your body wants to cave in, to take matters into your own hands. To follow the crowd, not the Rabbi from Nazareth.

David says, "Just wait. Life isn't over yet." But waiting is hard to do. That's why David's call is to "wait patiently" for the Lord.[2] Not for a man or a woman. Not for a proposal or a "yes." Not for a ring wrapped around your finger, but for God. And don't forget that God is with you, *right now*. You're not solitary. You're not alone. God is at your side through every En Gedi, every broken engagement, every rejection, every disappointment. He's there. You see, we're not just waiting *for* God. We're waiting *with* God.

Waiting is active, not passive. Notice the language. *Trust, do good, dwell, enjoy, take delight in, commit, be still*—seven staccato commands all leading up to "wait patiently" for the Lord. Each one is dripping with implications.

Trust in the Lord

To trust is to lean your weight on something. When you step out onto a bridge, you trust. You can do that with God. You lean your weight, your hopes, dreams, aspirations—all you are—on him. He can take the weight.

Do good

Don't let life *happen* to you. Do something with your life. Go to college. Travel the world. Get letters after your name. Write a novel. Start a business, a nonprofit—or both. Move to a poor part of town and serve those in need. Try something. Fail. Try again. Follow that part of your heart that you're scared to let out. Just do something *good*. Something that matters. Something that's about God's kingdom, not your comfort. Justice. Shalom. Partner with God for the healing of the world.

Life doesn't start when you get married. Or when you graduate or get a job or reach a goal—or whatever it is that you're waiting for. You're alive *now*. And life, as we all know, is evaporating. The biblical author James called it "a mist," like your breath on a February morning.[3] Waiting for the Lord doesn't mean sitting around, working a dead-end job, watching TV, or hoping Mr. or Ms. Right falls into your lap. It means beginning to do good right where you're at, and then watching your story unfold.

Dwell in the land

Sink your roots deep. Dig in. Don't bounce from job to job, city to city, relationship to relationship. Invest your life deeply, and be content.

What is contentment? It's when your life is *enough*. When you're satisfied with where you are, and when you are, and who you are. You don't covet another person's story. It's when you're enjoying the life God has spread out in front of you.

This is hard for me. I'm always thinking about what's next. Contentment is an elusive thing, isn't it? Maybe that's why the writer Paul says he *learned* to be content.[4] Because it's anything but the default setting for most of us. But you can learn to dwell. I am, and that's saying something.

Enjoy safe pasture

Do you *enjoy* your life? Or are you so focused on the future that you're missing out on the present? So obsessed with what you don't have that you forget what you do have? Life is a gift. Deeply enjoy every moment you can. Savor the ordinary. A cup of coffee. A meal with friends. A good night's sleep. Laughter. Plant your feet on the ground and take it all in. Because what you're doing now will set the stage for your future.

This phrase "enjoy safe pasture" can also be translated "cultivate faithfulness."[5] It's a farming metaphor. Before someone can plant (much less harvest) a crop, they have to get the soil ready. If it's hard and brittle, it's no good for growth. They have to tear it up in order to make it healthy and soft. The same is true of life. Before God can do whatever it is we're waiting for, we need to get our lives ready.

What about you? Ask yourself the hard questions. "Are my finances in order, or am I swimming in debt? Have I figured out a trajectory for my life, or am I just spinning my wheels at a meaningless job? Have I dealt with my past? Have I opened up my life to Jesus and his people and started the healing process, or am I just pretending that I'm fine?"

I know so many people who sit around dreaming about marriage, but if they met someone tomorrow, it would be *years* before they were ready to take that step.

Take delight in the Lord

What a great line. Notice it's a *command* — take delight in God. And when you take delight in God, when you look to him for satisfaction, fulfillment, meaning, purpose, identity, validation — all the things you look for in love or a marriage or a career or a dream — your desires *change*.

You think you're craving romance, but really you're craving God. You think you're dying to get married, but really it's God who is underneath your desires. You think you're waiting for _____ (you fill in the blank here), but really you're waiting for God.

This isn't a formula to manipulate God into giving you what you want. It's not saying that *if* you delight in God, *then* he will come through for you. No. This is about desire replacement. When you chase after God, more than any other thing, you will find that your desires for what you *don't* have, what you're waiting for, are replaced by the pleasure of what you *do* have, in God. When all of your heart is wrapped up in him, your desires change.

Commit your way to the Lord

Whatever is in front of you, wherever you're en route to, commit it to God. What does that mean? I think it means you make God your navigator. You pray, *"God, here's my map. Here's where I'm going. I think this path is from you. But if I'm wrong or need a course correction, stop me, redirect me, turn me around. You lead. I'll follow."*

This is something we should do *daily,* not just when we pick out a college or decide on a spouse. I cannot tell you how many mornings I wake up and pray, *"God, show me what to do."* And guess what? He does.

Be still before the Lord

Okay, this one is hard, at least for me. To say I'm impatient would be a gross understatement. I *can't stand* waiting. Put me in traffic, in a meeting, in line, and I crawl out of my skin. I'm impatient with people, with life, and with God. This is a massive weakness in my life. Tammy is the exact opposite. She is the embodiment of patience. It's a shining bright spot in her character, and it's one of my favorite things about her. She's *calm*. Every time I'm around her I relax. I'm a bit of an insomniac. At night my mind just won't settle down. On nights when I can't sleep, I just curl up against her back and match my breathing to hers — she's so *still*.

To be still is to slow down, take a deep breath, stop fidgeting, stop fighting, stop banging your head against the wall, and just *be* ...

Do that right now. Take a deep breath. Then be still for a moment.

See how good that feels?

Wait patiently for God

Finally, after getting all that out on the table, David writes, "And wait patiently for him."

Notice how much is crammed into that last phrase. The imagery isn't of a guy sitting in a waiting room, bored out of his mind, waiting for God to call his name. It's of trusting, doing, dwelling, enjoying, cultivating, delighting, committing — it's of a man or a woman walking with God into the future.

The reality is that there's so much work to be done right now.

Before you ever meet him or her, or get married. Before you graduate. Before you do *whatever.* There's so much that has to happen in your life to shape you into the kind of man or woman who's ready for that next step.

More important than finding your spouse is becoming the kind of person who's ready to get married. We expend so much time and energy dreaming about finding the perfect man or woman. But we can't control that. All we can do is work hard to become the kind of man or woman Jesus is calling us to be. The kind of man or woman for whom *someone* out there is waiting.

The odds are that you will marry somebody who is a mirror of your character. We all know exceptions to the rule, but they're just that—exceptions. If your faith is weak and apathetic, don't expect to marry someone who is filled with the Spirit of God and all-in for his kingdom. If you're not going anywhere with your life, don't expect to marry someone who is. If you're not saving your sexuality for marriage, don't expect that of your future spouse.

That's why the way you live now matters. *Right now you are becoming your future.* That's why the months or years or decades of waiting are so vital. You're building the foundation. And how you build, how you live in the here and now, matters more than you know.

David wrote, "Those who wait for the LORD, they will inherit the land."[6] There is a land—a life rich with God's blessing—that can be yours, but so much of it depends on waiting well.[7]

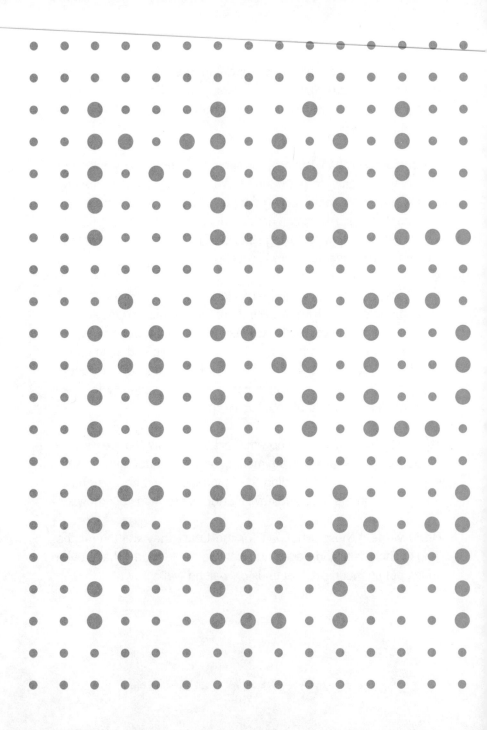

Part 5

Male and female

X and Y

God created human beings as "male and female." Not androgynous and asexual. We're not interchangeable. Every cell in our bodies is stamped XX or XY. Gender is literally in our DNA.

I'm not just a human. I'm a man. And God wanted it that way.

There's a sweeping movement in culture to erase gender. To argue that gender, or at least gender *roles*, is a "social construct" — something we made up over the years. As children, we grow up in an environment where we are forced to comply with an either-or dichotomy. Blue or pink. No yellow. And the time has come to emancipate humans from the tyrant Gender and his oppressive regime.

It makes sense. Thousands of years of toxic, anticreative, suffocating treatment of women has ignited a well-deserved backlash.

But I don't think we need to throw out the baby with the bathwater.

Gender is at the heart of what it means to be human. We read about gender on the opening page of the Scriptures. In fact, it's one of the first things we learn about this strange, new creature.

> So God created mankind in his own image,
>   in the image of God he created them;
>   male and female he created them.[1]

Part of what it means to be made "in the image of God" is that we are male and female. Both sexes image, or mirror, aspects of what God is like. Throughout the Scriptures, metaphorical language is used of God as both masculine and feminine. Yes, more often masculine is used. God is called "he," not "she." And he is a husband to Israel, father to the Messiah, king, warrior, and so on. But that doesn't mean God is a guy. The creator is also *El-Shaddai*, a woman giving birth, a nursing mother, and a hen with her chicks under her wings.[2] That means we need both sexes to do our job, to show the world what God is like.

Gender is central to our humanity. It isn't an add-on from after the fall that started around the Byzantine Era. From the beginning, *from the first sentence about human in the Bible*, we were male and female. If we abandon our gender or our gender roles (and in my mind the two are interconnected), we risk giving away a key part of our humanity. To lose it is to risk missing out on who God made you to be, and to find it is to discover a way to thrive.

Now, I'm well aware this may set off all the red lights on your dashboard. Gender roles — really, John Mark? I thought you were … smarter than that.

This is a tough subject to wade through. Maybe you've been abused by male (or female) gender roles. The victim of a power play. Or the perpetrator. There are very few pacifists in the gender war, and there is collateral damage all over the place. Maybe you were passed over for a promotion by a chauvinistic boss just because you were a woman. Or maybe your father made you feel like an embarrassment because you were lousy at sports.

If that's you, please take a deep breath and hear me out. There's no need to hyperventilate or throw down this book in disgust. Just listen for a bit. I'm gonna wade into some stuff that isn't crystal clear in the Scriptures. So I'll go easy. And if you're one of the lucky few for whom this *isn't* a touchy issue, don't tune out. As much as I would love to tiptoe around this subject, it's a vital step in getting back to the garden.

Equal, but unique

The first thing we learn about the sexes in *Genesis* is that we are equal. The ground is level between Adam and Eve.

We are both made in the image of God.

We are both called to "fill the earth and subdue it." To make culture. To shape the world into a gardenlike city.

We are both called to "be fruitful and increase in number." To fill up the earth with life.

And we both carry the curse, the exile from Eden.

This goes without saying in the modern world, but down through history the idea that women were equal to men was a new, subversive, radical, and freeing idea. Wherever the gospel has gone, it has done more to elevate the role of women than anything. I've heard it said that Jesus was the first feminist. It's not a bad line. The way he treated women was millennia ahead of his time. And not just Jesus. Historians think Paul was the first author in human history to argue that men and women were created equal. "There is neither Jew nor Gentile, neither slave nor free, nor is there male and female, for you are all one in Christ Jesus." [3] *Nobody* said that in the ancient world. Nobody says that in much of the modern world! Think about the difference between the role of women in the West, which has been deeply influenced by the church, and the Middle East or parts of Asia.

Whatever side of the world you live on, the Scriptures are adamant. Women are in no way, shape, or form inferior to men. We are equal in every way.

But we are also *unique*. In Adam's poem in Genesis 2, he states, "She shall be called 'woman,' for she was taken out of man." [4] In Hebrew, it's a wordplay. "She shall be called *ishah*, for she was taken out of *ish*." It's Adam's way of saying, "She's like me, but she's not like me at all. She's familiar, but she's different. Strange. Unique."

How are we different? Hmmm — dare I even try to answer that without degenerating into the stereotypes we all hate? Let's throw a few softballs first …

One obvious example is biologically. The doctor said, "It's a boy" seconds after I was born because I had ... well, boy stuff. This wasn't forced on me by culture. It was in my DNA from conception.

Another example is function. My maleness is more than just anatomy. Men were made to implant life into women in ways that women will never be able to. And women were made to nurture children in ways that men will never be able to. That's why you can't separate gender from gender roles. They overlap too much.

We see this play out in the aftermath of the fall. Adam is cursed in his relationship to the ground. Toil, sweat. Work is no longer an effortless joy. But Eve is cursed in her relationship to the family. Pain in childbearing.[5]

No matter how you read the Genesis story, that's gotta say *something* about who we are.

Now, very few people would disagree with this. The questions are, "What does this mean? What effect, if any, should this have on how I live? On what I do? On my marriage? Family? Church? Culture at large?" Those are the questions we can't seem to agree on. It's tricky. How do we know which differences are hardwired by God and which ones *are* a social construct? There are all sorts of stereotypes floating around culture. Which ones are from God and which ones aren't?

And it's confusing because we're caught in the crosscurrents of culture. One tide is saying there is *no difference* between the sexes and is working overtime to emasculate men and at the same time to erase the feminine side of women. The other current, which is just as strong, is pressuring us to fit into all sorts of stereotypes we don't relate to.

Think of the saying, "Stop crying and be a man!" What's unmanly about crying? Does "Jesus wept" ring a bell? And "be a man" — what does *that* even mean? There are a ton of stereotypes of masculinity in culture, so which one should I "be"?

Should I be the 007, stylish, tough, smooth, womanizing kind of man?

Or the NASCAR, drink-a-six-pack-every-night-and-work-on-my-Chevy man?

Or the Donald Trump, mogul, power suit, I-have-everything man?

Or the "my body is a temple" bro-man who spends every evening at 24 Hour Fitness looking at himself in the mirror?

What if I don't relate to any of the above? I live in Portland, which, I must admit, isn't exactly the epicenter of masculinity. There are a lot of guys with beards, but other than that, it's pretty tame. A few years ago, we were voted the least manly city in America.[6] A nationwide survey was done (don't people have anything better to do?), and we ranked at the bottom. Dead last. But listen to what the survey measured — the number of sports teams, hardware stores, home improvement stores, steak houses, pickup trucks, motorcycles, tools, and fishing licenses.

True story.

Your city was docked points based on the number of home furnishing stores, minivan sales, and subscription rates to beauty magazines.

So *this* is what it means to "be a man"? Going to Home Depot? Eating red meat? Driving a truck? Oh yeah, and whatever happens, *don't* cry.

Seriously?

What about the fact that it wasn't long ago when men were known more for art and poetry and music? It was a man who carved *David* and who painted Daniel on the Sistine Chapel ceiling. It was a man who put *Romeo and Juliet* on paper. And it was a man who composed *The Four Seasons*.

What if I like that stuff more than red meat and sports? In fact, what if I'm a vegetarian and I'm lousy at basketball? Does that make me less of a man?

And if anything, it's *worse* for women. The spectrum of options is even broader.

Should you be the smart, educated, I-have-my-act-together professional, with just a little bit of makeup but not too much?

Or the loyal, supportive, stay-at-home mom who packs her husband a brown-bag lunch every day?

Or the tan, model-thin, aloof sex goddess that men trip over?

Or the all-natural, outdoorsy, no-makeup-at-all girl who spends her days off hiking or juicing spirulina?

What if you're none of the above? What if you're smart and funny, and you want to start a business, but you also want to be a mom? And you like girl stuff, but you're not a six-foot skinny fashionista? Does that make you less of a woman?

The answer is no. Not at all. The trick is to eject the stereotypes imposed on you by culture while keeping your grip on the roles set in place by God.

So what *are* the roles? Once you clear away all the junk added in by culture, what's left?

As I see it, the answer is more of a story than a letter on a multiple-choice test. Here's the short version. In the beginning God made male and female, but he made Adam *first*. He set Adam in the garden, all by himself, to "work it and take care of it."[7] We have no idea how long he was alone. A day? A month? A year? There were a lot of animals that needed naming.

This is interesting. Why not make Adam and Eve at the same time? Why wait?

In the Hebrew worldview, the firstborn was the heir to the inheritance. He was no better than the other children. In fact, God loved to go around the firstborn at times and bless the youngest, just to invert the order and show who was really in charge. But as a general rule, the firstborn would lead the family or tribe or nation.

The apostle Paul brings this up in the New Testament. Whenever he writes anything about gender roles and why men should step up and lead, he goes back to *Genesis*. Paul's theology of gender roles is grounded in the creation story. He makes a big deal in 1 Corinthians 11 and 1 Timothy 2 about the fact that Adam was formed first. To Paul, there's an *order* in creation. God ordered the world, and then he put Adam in it. Adam ordered the garden, and then he put Eve in it. And that order is the template for us to work off of.

Remember that the Genesis story isn't just a one-off. Adam and Eve's marriage is a paradigm for *all marriages.* That's how I read it, in part because that seems to be how Jesus, and then later Paul, is reading it. If I'm right, that means Adam's firstness is more than a history lesson on ancient Hebrew culture. It's a God-designed order to follow.

And if you think I'm reading too much into one story, there are other signs pointing in the same direction. Eve is made from Adam, from his "rib." (Guys, don't let this go to your head. You were made from the dust.) Then she is named by Adam. "She shall be called woman." In the ancient Near East, naming was a sign of relationship and authority. Then at the end of the story, God states, "That is why *a man leaves his father and mother* [and his gaming system and free rent with his parents and his part-time job ...] ... and they become one flesh." Notice, it's the man who does the leaving, not the woman.

As I read all this evidence, it points to the idea that the man was made to be the leader in the marriage relationship. To clarify, by "lead" I do *not* mean "domineer." The word "lead" is so warped I'm not even sure if it works anymore. By "lead" I mean "give your life away for the good of another." Jesus is the paradigm for leadership. We'll get into more detail in the next chapter. For now, think of Adam as the leader.

Eve, on the other hand, is made as Adam's *ezer,* his partner. She's the one who comes alongside to get the job done. Her role is vital. Adam is incapable by himself. Without her, the whole thing falls apart.

I repeat, she is *indispensable.*

He is not enough all alone.

And just to clarify, everything I'm saying has to do with male-female relationships in *marriage*—not in culture at large.[8] The Scriptures have nothing to say about who should be the president of the

United States or the CEO of a company. This is about how we relate to one another from the wedding day forward.

Man does have a special connection to work. He's put in the garden "to work it and take care of it," and then he's cursed in the field. And woman does have a special connection to the family. She's called "the mother of all the living,"[9] and then she's cursed in childbearing. Yet *both* men and women are called to rule over the earth (work) and be fruitful and increase in number (family). Man is just called to lead the way.

It's that simple. Controversial, divisive, incendiary, yes — but simple. The man was made to lead, and the woman to be his partner, right at his side.

But notice how vague the "roles" are. There are all sorts of space and room and openness in how we express and live out this idea of the man as the leader and the woman as the partner. Other than the generic stuff about work and family, there's so much freedom to work out your gender roles in your marriage, church, culture, and time. The Scriptures give very few specifics.

Who should do the finances in a marriage? Is it okay for women to work outside the home? How much? What about stay-at-home dads? How should a couple make decisions when they don't agree? What if the husband doesn't follow Jesus?

The Bible doesn't say.

As a general rule, where the Bible is dogmatic, we should be dogmatic. Where the Bible is ambiguous, we should be open-minded and loaded with grace. And where the Bible is silent, we should shut the heck up.

So often we import cultural bias into the text and then claim it's "biblical." This happens all the time with gender, especially in the American church. The mid-twentieth-century American stereotype of Beaver's mom stuck at home with high heels on all day long has absolutely zero grounding in the Scriptures. Read Proverbs 31. The archetype of a Hebrew wife isn't chained to the kitchen stove. She's an entrepreneur, a real estate investor, a generous justice advocate, a loving mother, and a fashionista who hits the ground running before the sun even comes up. It says nothing about an apron.

We forget that prior to recent history, men and women both worked. Usually the children worked as well. Only the rich could live on one income. The difference was that the family worked on the farm or in the shop, not in an office across town. Still, we have to be *really* careful not to read our culture into the Bible's commands.

The Bible is transcultural. It was written at a specific time and to a specific place, but it's *for* all time, all places. That's why all the stuff about gender is at thirty thousand feet. There are barely any specifics on what a man and woman should and shouldn't do in marriage, family, and the rest. Any of you who are rule people, I know you hate this. "Just tell me *what to do!*" I get it. But the Bible is that way by purpose, not by accident. That's why it works for people all over the world, thousands of years after it was written down.

The gender roles are more of a trajectory than a list of dos and don'ts. They're a compass pointing you in the right direction rather than a map.

I have my opinions about marriage and family and the church and who should and shouldn't do what. But often that's all they are — opinions. My goal isn't to sway you to my "position." To be honest, I would love to be wrong on this one. My position is *not* the hip, forward-thinking, progressive take. Among other thinkers my age, and especially in a city like Portland, I'm the odd man out. But for me, this is about the Bible. Personally, I don't see any other way to read the Scriptures. When it comes to gender roles, I think the church is more often a mirror of culture than a prophetic voice to culture. And I think it's only a matter of time until it comes back to bite us. I mean, if God set it up this way, then it's for a reason. So feel free to disagree with me. Lots of smart, educated, Jesus-loving people do. That's fine. But at least think about it. What if I'm right?

Here's the hill I die on. We're not unisex. We're male and female. And that's a good thing.

War, peace, and why marriage is really about Jesus

There's a growing movement inside the church to say that gender roles are a result of the fall. From my vantage point, nothing could be further from the truth. Gender roles are a part of the original Edenic, good creation. But the gender *wars*? Those are a result of the fall. Absolutely.

In Eden, the serpent temped Eve, not Adam. In doing so, he was going around God's order, usurping God's authority. And instead of leading his wife, Adam followed his wife — into sin. It was the *exact opposite* of what was supposed to happen. A reversal of the roles. An inversion of the order.

And the result is catastrophic. God says to Eve, "Your desire will be for your husband, and he will rule over you."[1] Before the fall, man's role was just to lead, but ever since Genesis 3, man's bent has been to domineer, to subjugate, and to objectify women.

And what is history but proof that this prophecy is true? Men were made to lead, but because of sin, some men abuse that leadership and are oppressive, while other men abdicate that leadership (in rebellion against God) and are passive. We see this in men who are lazy or unmotivated. Ironically, this was Adam's sin. He stood by and allowed the serpent to twist God's words. Domineering men get all the attention, but I would argue that for every domineering alpha male there are countless passive men who do nothing.

We live right in the middle of this ongoing war. This is not how God set it up. This is not Eden, but this is the world we call home. And it's one of the reasons we see so much controversy around gender roles. We don't want to "submit" to anyone, much less a husband or wife. To say we're "antiauthoritarian" would be the understatement of the century. We value individual freedom above all.

But in this war, we're torn. We keep falling in love with the enemy. Because men and women are different, we don't understand each other. We get mad, frustrated, hurt, and angry. But because we're unique, we're also drawn to one another. We see the opposite sex as strange, captivating, exotic, and alluring. We live in this catch-22.

We can't abandon gender roles because of all the tension and abuse and pain over the years. If we do, we'll miss out on a central part of our humanity. Gender roles aren't "oppressive." Men are — and so are women at times. Gender roles are *good*. We don't need freedom from the roles. We need healing between men and women.

And while healing is found in Jesus, not in a husband or wife, marriage is a life-giving place to explore and experience that healing and to model the return to Eden.

Hypotasso

The writer Paul has a famous passage about marriage in his letter to the Ephesians. Some people love it. Others think it should be torn out of the Bible. It's provocative and dangerous and, well, one of a kind. He begins by writing, "Submit to one another out of reverence for Christ."[2]

This word *submit* is *hypotasso* in Greek, and it can be translated "respect" or "yield" or "defer" or "put another's good ahead of your own." It does *not* mean "do what you're told." It means "give your feelings, desires, and trust over to another." And *both* men and women are called to do this. The word *hypotasso* is used all over the New Testament epistles. Children are to submit to parents. Followers of Jesus are to submit to the elders of the church. Citizens are to submit to the government. Angels are to submit to God. This word has to do with order, with the way God set creation up to thrive.

That's why it gets Paul into so much trouble. Right after calling all followers of Jesus to submit to one another, he writes about what this looks like in marriage. This is the most in-depth teaching on marriage in the whole Bible, and the first thing Paul states is, "Wives, submit yourselves to your own husbands as you do to the Lord. For the husband is the head of the wife as Christ is the head of the church, his body, of which he is the Savior. Now as the church submits to Christ, so also wives should submit to their husbands in everything."[3]

Wow.

Sisters, take a deep breath. Before you freak, keep reading. Paul's not done. Next he writes to the husbands — "Husbands, love your wives, just as Christ loved the church and gave himself up for her to make her holy, cleansing her by the washing with water through the word, and to present her to himself as a radiant church ... In this same way, husbands ought to love their wives as their own bodies. He who loves his wife loves himself. After all, no one ever hated their own body, but they feed and care for their body, just as Christ does the church — for we are members of his body ... This is a profound mystery — but I am talking about Christ and the church. However, each one of you also must love his wife as he loves himself, and the wife must respect her husband."[4]

We read Paul's letter to the Ephesians and think the part about wives is scandalous, but in the first century, it would have been the exact opposite. The part about husbands would have been staggering for the men in the church. This is the Roman Empire in the AD 60s. All you owed your wife was a roof over her head and sperm for her children. If you're a husband, you're thinking, "Now you're telling me that I actually have to love her? To put her good above my own? To give my life for her? My time, my money, my freedom, my desires for her? To nourish her? To feed her physically *and* spiritually?"

Trust me, this letter would have created drama in Ephesus.

It's interesting that Paul says *twice* as much to the husbands as to the wives. The wives get three verses, and the husbands get nine. Why? Because the men are *the leaders*. God holds the men responsible to lead a healthy marriage. To God, authority is about responsibility, not bossing people around. Think of Adam and Eve in Genesis 3. Eve is the first one to take a bite from the fruit of the tree, but Adam is the first one to get in trouble. God says, "Where are you?" — as if to say, "What have you done?"[5] God holds Adam responsible.

But notice to whom the commands are written in *Ephesians*, because it's crucial.

"*Wives*, submit yourselves to your own husbands ..."

"*Husbands*, love your wives ..."

Nowhere is the man called to enforce the wife's role. "Husbands, make sure your wives submit to you." It doesn't say that. The husband is called to love, give, sacrifice, nourish, and put his wife's needs ahead of his own. That's all. And frankly, if men actually did that, I think there would be a truce in the gender wars.

And Paul never says, "Wives, make sure your husbands love you and treat you well." He just says the wife is called to submit, to yield, to come under the authority of and entrust herself to her husband. But submission is *her* choice. It is a gift that a wife gives to her husband of her own free will, with no force or coercion. And just to clarify, these roles are for *marriage*, not for culture at large. It's a gift she gives to her *husband*, not to all men.

Marriage is a safe place for men and women to return to the garden and work together to show the world the image of God. To show the world how captivating God really is.

Maybe you're thinking, "Okay, I get that God is loving, but God is submissive?" Yes, in a way.

At the end of the passage, Paul writes, "I am talking about Christ and the church." This whole thing is a picture of Jesus. Jesus is the example for both the man and the woman.

For the man, he's the picture of self-sacrifice, giving away his life on the cross, all in love.

But for the woman, he's the picture of joyful, eager, trusting submission to the Father. Remember Jesus in Gethsemane? After venting his feelings to God, he says, "Yet not my will, but yours be done."[6] It's hard, but he submits—he yields.

When a man doesn't want to give up his life for his wife, and a woman doesn't want to submit to her husband, then both of them are saying, in essence, "I don't want to be like Jesus." But the reverse is also true. Men and women both get a chance to play the Jesus role in marriage. Women through submission, and men through loving in a self-giving way. This is why Paul says marriage is a "profound mystery."

When a man is actually like Jesus in a marriage—when he loves, gives, nourishes—who doesn't want to submit to *that*?

And when a woman is actually like Jesus in a marriage—when she submits with joy and respect—what man on the planet doesn't want to make sacrifices for *that*?

Marriage is a place where Jesus' healing power is at work to set people free from thousands of years of fighting between the sexes and from all the wounding we carry from the war.

The same is true of the church. The church should be a place of freedom. A place where men are free to be men, and women to be women. With no guilt. No shame. And no pressure. Where the sexes are free from the culture's overpowering, hypercontrolling, oppressive view of what a man or a woman should or shouldn't be like. The church should be a safe place to be who God made you to be.

Sadly, rather than a place of freedom, the church has often been a place of strife and division and anger and angst. Some in the church have used the Bible to oppress women, to keep women out of so many things. The word *hierarchical* comes to mind. As much as I want to deny it, it's been true of the church for a long time. But others have been sucked right into the temptation to eradicate gender roles all together.

Listen, gender is something we should celebrate, not bicker and grumble about.

Remember Mark 10? Jesus' argument with the Pharisees about divorce? Don't forget what Jesus said. "It was because your hearts were hard that Moses wrote you this law [the one that stated a man could divorce his wife] ... But at the beginning of creation God 'made them male and female.'"[7] To Jesus, one of the reasons marriage is breaking down all over the place is that we lost sight of the fact that we were made male and female. When we jettison God's vision for relationships, we pay a steep price.

That's why the message of Jesus is good news. In and through Jesus there's a re-creation going on. Men and women are finding a new way to be human by living Jesus' way. It's anything but easy. Sometimes it's three steps forward and two steps back. But we're on the way out of the gender wars and into the kingdom of God. And if you're not, well, feel free to come along.

The gift that nobody wants

I asked my wife to marry me on Christmas Eve. When we were dating, we used to go driving in the hills outside the city. It was a chance to get out of town — to escape all the noise and traffic and to just be together and talk.

That chilly December night, I pulled over and asked her to walk out to an overlook. I'm sure we were trespassing on some farmer's land, but I was too young to care. And there, underneath a massive oak tree and overlooking all the city lights, I asked her to be my wife ... and she said yes — *thank God.*

Now every Christmas Eve we think about that night. It's such a warm memory. The kind that makes me smile whenever it comes to mind. For some reason, Christmas has always been a romantic time for me. Maybe it's because I kissed a woman for the first time that night on the hill. Or maybe it's because love is a gift.

Perhaps that's why when a couple is in love, they are filled with a childlike joy. They can't stop smiling. They forget to eat, and they can't sleep, breathe right, focus, or pay attention. Remember when you were a kid? That feeling of trying to fall asleep the night before Christmas? It was torture, but the pain was so good! Love is like that. It's like Christmastime. And the wedding day is like Christmas morning.

There's a line in *Proverbs* that reads, "He who finds a wife finds what is good and receives favor from the LORD."[1] I'm living proof of that. My wife is evidence of favor.

Marriage is hard work, long hours, and it's anything but heaven on earth — but it's a gift.

Having said that, I need to clarify that *singleness is a gift as well.*

There's a whole chapter in the Bible written to people who aren't married.[2] It's in *1 Corinthians*, one of several letters Paul wrote to the church in Corinth.[3] About halfway through, Paul starts fielding questions from the Corinthians. And guess what the questions were about? Loveology. There were questions about *porneia*, sex between married couples, marriage, divorce, and, of course, singleness. After all, the church was made up of followers of Jesus, and *Jesus was single.* This is interesting. As followers of Jesus, our agenda is to become more and more like our Rabbi. In light of that, should we get married at all?

Paul's answer is surprising. He writes, "I wish that all of you were as I am [single]. But each of you has your own gift from God; *one has this gift, another has that.*"[4]

To Paul, marriage is a gift, and *singleness is a gift.*

You may want the gift, but not have the gift.

You may have the gift, but not want the gift.

You may have the gift for a time, but not forever.

Or you may be widowed or divorced and get the gift later in life.

The word *gift* is *charisma* in Greek, from which we get the English word *charismatic*. It's a drive, a passion to do something. But it's also from the root word *charis*, meaning "grace." In Paul's theology, grace is way more than God saying he's cool with you. Grace is God's empowering presence deep in your bones, animating you from the inside out to do what he's put in front of you. And this language of *charisma* or *gift* is used all over Paul's writings. It's a calling and ability to participate in God's kingdom in a special and unique way.

The "gift of singleness" doesn't necessarily mean you don't want to get married. Scholars speculate that Paul was a widower.[5] Maybe he missed married life. Maybe not. Either way, just because you have a calling and ability from God to live a single life doesn't mean you don't desire marriage.

And it doesn't mean singleness is easy for you. It may be challenging. I have the gift of teaching. I believe it's what God put me on the planet to do. To be honest, it's the hardest thing I've ever done. It's labor. It's brutal at times. And more often than not, it's discouraging. However, there's something deep inside me that says, "I was made to do this."

Here's what you need to understand. *Singleness is a good thing.*

Really. The word *charisma* can be translated "blessing." It's not a curse. And it's not plan B.

In the church, sometimes we make people who aren't married feel like they're on the JV team. Like they never really "made it." If you're in your twenties and single, the odds are people ask you *all the time*, "Are you dating anybody? Do you like anybody? *Know* anybody?" And people are well-meaning, but the subliminal message is, "When are you going to get married and start life like the rest of us?"

But life doesn't start when you get married. It starts the second you fold your story into the larger kingdom and follow Jesus forward. *And Jesus was single!* So was Paul, the leading theologian in the New Testament. That's saying something. And both of these men see singleness as a gift.

This is all the more shocking when you get a handle on first-century culture. In the ancient Mediterranean, family was *everything*. In Jewish culture, if a man died with no "seed," people thought he was cursed by God. In Greco-Roman culture (like in Corinth), if a man died without having any children, people thought he died twice, because he was forgotten. In a sense, he vanished.

Caesar Augustus actually passed a law that fined widows who didn't remarry within two years. Seriously. There was a crushing pressure to marry young, and if your spouse died, to remarry as fast as you can.

And practically speaking, your children were your retirement plan. There were no social security checks or IRAs. Your children would take care of you when you could no longer work. That's how it was done for thousands of years, and still is in much of the world today.

Singleness was a radical idea in Paul's time. To stay single was to carry a stigma for your whole life and to risk dying in abject poverty. But not only was singleness okay in the early church. It was encouraged! Historians argue the early church was the first movement ever to hold out singleness as a viable way of life.

How could Paul think that way?

The answer is a few paragraphs later in 1 Corinthians 7. He goes on to clarify—"What I mean, brothers and sisters, is that *the time is short*. From now on those who have wives should live as if they do not; those who mourn, as if they did not; those who are happy, as if they were not; those who buy something, as if it were not theirs to keep; those who use the things of the world, as if not engrossed in them. *For this world in its present form is passing away*."[6]

Okay, pay close attention. This next part is slippery. Lots of people misunderstand what Paul is saying. He's *not* saying Jesus is coming back any second. If that was the case, then Paul was wrong. It's been a long time since he dropped *1 Corinthians* in the mail. And he's *not* saying Jesus is going to come back to blow up the planet and take everybody away to heaven in the clouds.[7]

Paul is saying we live at the convergence of two ages. Before Paul was the apostle we know and love, he was a well-known Jewish rabbi. And like the rabbis of that day, he separated human history into two ages — "this age" and "the age to come." "This age" was the world we're living in now. It was marked by the aftereffects of the fall — sin, death, pain, suffering, injustice, natural disasters, and the rest. "The age to come" was the future day, on the horizon, when God would break into human history and put everything right. God's Messiah, or King, would usher in a renewed, gardenlike world, and all would be well.

But Jesus is a curveball. His death and resurrection inaugurated the age to come *right in the middle* of this present age. Because of Jesus' coming, we don't live in this present age anymore — in the time of Abraham, Isaac, and Jacob, when you could settle down, start a family, and enjoy life. But neither do we live in the age to come, when the world will be set free from sin's grip.

Instead, we live in a time of conflict. Tension. We live at the fulcrum point of human history. In the overlap. This world (and by that Paul doesn't mean planet earth — he means the world system out of sync with God) in its present form *is* passing away, right now as we speak. And a new world is being born. We live on the cusp, right on the edge of this new reality. We live during an in-breaking of the future.

In light of this, Paul's question is simple. *Which world should we be living for — the one that is passing away, or the one that is coming to pass?*

The answer is obvious.

But living for the world that is coming means we need to rethink *everything*. Starting with marriage. "From now on those who have wives should live as if they do not ..." That doesn't mean I should be a lousy husband. It simply means my wife and I need to live for something greater than the American Dream.

This is something we all have to wrestle with. *Especially* if we're not married yet. We have to ask the hard questions. "Should I get married or not? If so, when?" "And what should my marriage look like in light of the in-breaking rule of God?"

That's why Paul's letter to the Corinthians is indispensable. He spends the better part of a chapter working out the answers. To guide you through the text, here are six questions you need to ask yourself before you get married. Each one is rooted in 1 Corinthians 7.

Let's start with the overt one ...

Do you have the gift of singleness?

Do you have the calling and ability from God to live single *in order to serve God in a greater capacity*? Make sure you get that last part. For followers of Jesus, the point of singleness isn't freedom from responsibility. It's freedom *for more* responsibility. Paul thinks it's great if you stay single. At the end of the chapter he says he thinks it's "better" than marriage. But Paul isn't saying you should abdicate responsibility, work part-time, go surfing every day, travel a bit, play in a band that never goes anywhere, and do nothing but chill for ten years of your life. Does that sound anything like the gospel to you? To Paul, the point of singleness is to serve God in ways you can't if you're married.

A friend of mine said no to dating an amazing girl because he wanted to live in the developing world for a few years. He's an engineer, and he took a job with a nonprofit, building wells in Mozambique. For three years he lived on the back of a motorcycle, traveling from village to village. At night he would camp in the bush, and then each day he would show people how to get clean water. It was an amazing experience, but it would have been really hard to do with a wife and family. He made a smart decision to do that as a single person in order to follow God's call.[8]

If you have this gift, even if you just have it for a while, then don't waste time pining after romance. Do what God has put in your heart.

Will marriage help me or hold me back from God's calling on my life?

Paul writes, "A married man is concerned about the affairs of this world — how he can please his wife — and his interests are divided. An unmarried woman or virgin is concerned about the Lord's affairs: Her aim is to be devoted to the Lord in both body and spirit ... I am saying this for your own good, not to restrict you, but that you may live in a right way in undivided devotion to the Lord."[9]

Remember that all healthy marriages are centered around a calling, a mission, a job, a task. The point of marriage *isn't marriage*, especially in light of the time in which we live. There's an urgency to life—to see the kingdom come to bear on our world.

That's why you need to ask these questions—"What has God put in my heart? What am I called to? What's my mission in life?" And ideally you should ask these questions before you get married, because you have to be on the same page.

What has God put in front of you? Will marriage help you do that, or will it make it harder? If God is calling you to live out the gospel in Syria, where you could face torture and even death, then maybe marriage isn't a smart idea. I'm not sure you should drag a family into that. But if God has called you to, say, live out the gospel in Portland or LA, then maybe marriage will fuel you. I couldn't do what I do without my wife. Over half of our church is female. I need her wisdom, her insight, her help.

If marriage pulls you away from God's calling on your life, then slow down. You may be on the wrong trajectory.

Do you burn?

Paul advises, "Now to the unmarried and the widows I say: It is good for them to stay unmarried, as I do. But if they cannot control themselves, they should marry, for it is better to marry than to burn with passion ... If anyone is worried that he might not be acting honorably toward the virgin he is engaged to, and if his passions are too strong and he feels he ought to marry, he should do as he wants. He is not sinning. They should get married."[10]

Remember this is first-century Corinth. It's a different world from the one you and I know. Marriage was more about functionality than love. There was a school of heavyweight philosophers in Paul's day called the Stoics. They said you should marry for family, for children, and for business, never for love.

But Paul's no Stoic. He says, in essence, "If you're in love, and you can barely keep your hands in your pockets, then get married. Go ahead." In fact, that's one of the ways you know you *don't* have the gift of singleness. You "burn." "To burn" is a Greek euphemism for raging sexual desire.

This is a huge issue today. Technology has changed the world, for the better *and the worse*. In Paul's day, there was no Internet porn, no trashy advertisements on the side of the road, and no smut in the checkout lane at the grocery store. And the average couple married at fourteen or fifteen years old. Today, temptation is greater than it's ever been and we're waiting more than a decade longer to marry. That's a dangerous mixture. And while I don't think we should tell high schoolers to run out and get married, I do think marriage is more important than ever before. If you "burn," marriage is the God-created venue in which to express your sexuality.

Is now the right time?

Paul goes on to say, "Because of the present crisis, I think that it is good for a man to remain as he is. Are you pledged to a woman? Do not seek to be released. Are you free from such a commitment? Do not look for a wife. But if you do marry, you have not sinned ... But those who marry will face many troubles in this life, and I want to spare you this."[11]

This text is really hard to interpret because we're not sure what the "present crisis" is. Reading *1 Corinthians* is kind of like listening to one side of a phone conversation — we end up guessing what's on the other side. The leading theory is that there was a serious shortage of food in Corinth. Right around the time Paul wrote *1 Corinthians*, two major famines were occurring in southern Greece. In the ancient world, famines were dangerous times of social unrest. Think of what's going on in parts of North Africa and the Middle East right now. In times of crisis, it's hard enough to feed one mouth, much less two.

So there are times when it's really not a good idea to get involved with someone, much less to get married.

If you're in the middle of a crisis. If you live in Egypt or North Korea right now.

If you're dealing with a tragedy. The death of a family member. The trauma of sin. You're not in a healthy spot. You're not yourself during times like these.

If you're in college. You can get married in college. I did. It's not sin. It's just hard. You will start off well below the poverty line and unsure of what's coming. We made it through, but there were a few bumpy spots along the way.

If you're new in your career and you're working a hundred hours a week with no time for relationships. You're just trying to keep your head above water, so it's probably not a smart time to plunge into marriage.

You're free to get married at any time. Marriage is a good thing! If you marry, "You have not sinned." (Thanks Paul, we were worried about that.) But make sure you think it through. Don't rush in. Is it the intelligent thing to do? Or is it the right thing at the wrong time?

Can you see yourself with him or her for the rest of your life?

Toward the end of the chapter Paul writes, "A woman is bound to her husband as long as she lives ..."[12]

Not for the near future.

Not for a decade.

Not for "as long as I'm happy, and if not, well, we have the prenup."

Marriage is for "as long as we both shall live." That's a *long* time. Fifty or sixty years, if all goes well. Can you see yourself together at seventy, eighty, ninety years of age? When all the euphoria of young love has faded? When you can't even see or hear each other anymore? And if so, does that idea excite you? Do you want to grow old together?

This is a question you need to wrestle with long and hard. It's important. It's *for life*.

Does he or she "belong to the Lord"?

In the second-to-the-last verse of the chapter, Paul writes, "If her husband dies, she is free to marry anyone she wishes, but he must belong to the Lord."

He must belong to the Lord.

This one isn't hard to understand, but it can be hard to swallow. Paul is saying, "Don't even *think* about marrying someone who isn't a follower of Jesus." That's not an option, no matter what you *feel*. This means you shouldn't even think about flirting with, much less dating, somebody who's not on the same page as you in faith.

My wife spends a ton of time with young women in our church who aren't yet married. She's a walking wisdom dispenser, and smart people always want to get her thoughts on life. On a regular basis I hear her say, "You can't choose who you fall in love with, but you can choose who you spend time with." She's right. The heart has a mind of its own. You can't dictate or script your feelings. You can't decide in advance who you will "fall" for. But you *can* decide who you will see, hang around, think about, talk to, and be around.

That's why *Proverbs* reads, "Above all else, guard your heart." [13] Watch out for intruders, for people who get under your skin — into your thinking and feeling — but shouldn't be there.

This is an issue that Paul keeps harping on with the Corinthians. In his second letter, he makes the exact same point, but with an even louder voice: "Do not be yoked together with unbelievers. For what do righteousness and wickedness have in common? Or what fellowship can light have with darkness? What harmony is there between Christ and Belial? Or what does a believer have in common with an unbeliever?" [14]

"Yoked together" is a farming analogy from the ancient world. You would never yoke together two different kinds of animals — like a donkey with an ox or a horse with a camel. If you did, the animals would start off okay, but pretty soon they would pull at two different speeds in two different directions, and the tension would either tear your cart to pieces or drive it off course.

That's what happens when a believer in Jesus is "yoked" to an unbeliever. Since you pull in two different directions, it's only a matter of time until your relationship will go off track or, worse yet, implode.

If you're a follower of Jesus, your faith is at the core of your being. It's what drives you. You will never be able to walk in sync with someone who doesn't believe what you believe and live how you live. They will always think you are strange. No matter how much they respect you, they will never understand you.

I know this may be really hard to hear. The thought of having to choose between your lover and your God is gut-wrenching. That's why Paul quotes the prophet Isaiah a couple of verses later. "Come out from them and be separate ... I will be a Father to you, and you will be my sons and daughters, says the Lord Almighty."[15] That's God's way of saying, "I will satisfy your relational needs. What you're craving can be found in me."

We think we have to get married in order to experience relational life. But that's not true. We're sons and daughters of God, and that means we're brothers and sisters. We have the family of God, the church, as a place to invest deeply in relationships. In fact, when you're single, you can actually have *more* relationships.

That's why singleness is good. So good that Paul calls it a gift. You may have the gift, or you may not, but either way, you can find life in God and his family.

The closing line in 1 Corinthians 7 is, "In my judgment, she is happier if she stays as she is — and I think that I too have the Spirit of God."

She's *happier*? Unmarried? Paul thinks the answer is yes. Because happiness or life or joy — or whatever we want to call it — is about so much more than romance. So many romantic movies end with marriage, and that's fine, but marriage isn't the end goal of life.

The point of living is to do what you were *made to do*. To live for God's world that's already taking root, not for the one that's fading off the scene. And to live with "undivided devotion to the Lord."[16]

Gay

You've made it this far.

That says something about you — grit, determination, moxie. Well done.

We've been on this journey together through the Scriptures, getting a picture of God's vision for *ahava*. From the beginning, it was a man and a woman coming together to "rule," to take the world forward … *echad*, fused together as one, reconnecting that bond over and over again through the pleasure of sex … "naked and unashamed," vulnerable, safe with each other … the dance of giving and receiving, dying and rising, just like Jesus … and bound together by faithfulness, not for a year, or three, or until the emotions wind down, but for life.

It's a pretty compelling vision, isn't it?

But there are other visions. The fall mucked everything up. It made God's vision blurry to human eyes. We started thinking we could do better. We started repainting, coming up with our own picture of what could be. What should be. With an alternate vision.

A little bit of Adam and Eve goes a long way.

Sin warped our understanding of God's vision for human sexuality. There's a profound line in the opening chapter of Paul's letter to the Romans, where he's talking about what happened when humanity turned away from God. We "worshiped and served created things rather than the Creator." Paul writes, "Therefore God gave them over in the sinful desires of their hearts to sexual impurity for the degrading of their bodies with one another."[1]

In Paul's retelling of the Genesis story, the first thing that happened after the fall is our sexuality is thrown out of joint. And then he gives a graphic example. "Because of this, God gave them over to shameful lusts. Even their women exchanged natural sexual relations for unnatural ones. In the same way the men also abandoned natural relations with women and were inflamed with lust for one another."[2]

The label *homosexuality* is less than a hundred years old. It was first used by German psychologists, who divided all humans into two categories based on their sexual orientation — *hetero* or *homo*. But same-sex attraction is nothing new. *Romans* was written a long time ago.

And this alternate vision, this repainting of what could and should be, is *the* issue of our day. You can ignore it, close your eyes and pretend it's not there, and hope it goes away, or you can yell at it, lambast it, and throw rocks at it — but it's not going anywhere. This is something we *have* to talk about.

For me, though, this isn't an "issue."

It's Matthew, my friend who left the church to express his sexuality with other men. He was forced to pick between Jesus and his sexuality. He chose his sexuality.

It's Alex, who never thought of herself as gay but just confessed to my wife and me that the reason she disappeared from church a year ago was because she started having sex with her roommate. When her roommate moved out, she was hurt and confused.

It's Ezra, a guy in our church who has been attracted to men as long as he can remember but grew up in an angry, fundamentalist church. He has one foot in the gay world, which is often anti-Christian, and one foot in the church, which is often anti-gay, and he's spent the last decade oscillating between the two. He doesn't feel at home in either.[3]

It's the countless conversations with gay people I've had, who, the second they find out I work for a church, wall up, shut down, and break off the conversation.

It's people all around me in my church, my neighborhood, my city — family, friends, loved ones — who are all trying to figure out how to reconcile the call of Jesus with the pull of sexual desire.

For me, this isn't about politics. It's about people. People I love and care about.

Which is why I want to start off with an apology. If you're gay, this is for you. There is no "official" voice for "the church," and if there was, it wouldn't be me, but I know I speak for millions of Jesus followers when I say this — *we are so very sorry for the way we have treated you.*

In our quest to hold on to God's vision of marriage and sexuality, we lost our grip on God's heart. We became the very thing Jesus stood against. Mean. Malignant. Vicious at times. The caricature of Jesus followers as homophobic, narrow-minded, and intolerant has been true far too often. Horrible things have been said in the name of Jesus. Damaging, hurtful, abusive words have come from men like me, men who claim to speak for God. In the process, we have pushed away the very people Jesus called to himself. We have been blind to our own hypocrisy. We have been slow to listen and quick to speak. And we have done so much damage to people's view of God.

I live in the first city in America to have an openly gay mayor. A while back he organized a meeting with ten city leaders — five from the church and five from the LGBT community. We sat in his office at city hall and just talked. My friend Rick, who leads an amazing church in town called Imago Dei, started the dialogue with an apology.[4] He said, "We repent of the things we've done to you in the name of Jesus."

I loved how he used that word *repent.* It's fitting, don't you think?

It was crushing for me to listen to the stories of these people. One woman said, "The most hurtful things I've ever had said about me came from behind a pulpit." My heart dropped through the floor. I was surprised by how many of these leaders had a background in the church (in Portland, that's rare). And not one of them had anything good to say about Jesus' people. Could I really blame them?

Put simply, we in the church have not been like Jesus, and we sincerely apologize. *Please* don't hold the sins of the church against him.

Now let me be clear about what I believe. God's vision of marriage between a man and a woman is the venue for love and sexuality. I believe that's the *best* vision for human flourishing, and that all other visions — homosexual *or heterosexual* — are a parody of what God spoke into existence all those years ago.

I love this vision because I love the God I'm convinced is giving it to me. To *all* of us. But so often this "issue" is no more than a shouting match, with the church on one side and the LGBT community on the other, lobbing grenades at each other.

In this shouting match, I believe that both sides don't always tell the truth. There are myths that have sunk deep into the Western psyche that just aren't right. Some of them even come from inside the church. Here are six of them, as I see it.

Myth 1: Gay sex is the worst sin ever

The first myth is that, on the scale of bad to worse, homosexuality is at the top. On the sin-o-meter, so the myth goes, this one is blinking emergency red.

It's always stupid to play the sin-rating game. We inevitably rank the sins we don't struggle with at the top, and the ones we do struggle with as "not that bad." It's all too easy for me to slam men having sex with men because I'm attracted to women and I'm happily married. I can express my sexuality anytime I want. It's easy for me to say homosexuality is worse than lust or fantasy or not treating my wife well. That makes me feel better about myself.

But at the end of the day, does it really matter whose sin is worse? It's still sin, and it still causes pain and damage to people we love.

Later in *Romans*, Paul writes, "There is no difference between Jew and Gentile, for all have sinned and fall short of the glory of God."[5] None of us measure up. We *all* fall short. Does it really matter who falls short by a few feet, and who by a few miles? Isn't Paul's point that we *all* fall short?

Jew, Gentile.

Gay, straight.

We *all* need Jesus.

Don't get me wrong, some sins *are* worse than others. The writer John says, "There is a sin that leads to death," and there is "a sin that does not lead to death."[6] Murder is worse that gossip, for sure. *But both are wrong.* John ends by saying, "All wrongdoing is sin." That's what I'm trying to say.

This idea of homosexuality as the "worst" sin comes from a misreading of Romans 1. Some claim that Paul is laying out the downward spiral of sin, and homosexuality is at the bottom. Part of that is true. Paul *is* tracing the downward spiral of what happens when a culture turns away from God. We worship the creation rather than the Creator, we live with a spirit of entitlement (we call it "rights" today), rather than gratitude, and as a result, we become obsessed with ourselves. And it is also true that Paul uses gay and lesbian sex as a graphic example of that inversion. It's a telling sign that a culture has said no to God and his design for creation.

However, it's *not* the end of the spiral. There's a whole other paragraph we often skip right over. Paul follows up by saying, "Furthermore,... God gave them over to a depraved mind ... They have become filled with every kind of wickedness, evil, greed and depravity. They are full of envy, murder, strife, deceit and malice. They are gossips, slanderers, God-haters, insolent, arrogant and boastful; they invent ways of doing evil; they disobey their parents; they have no understanding, no fidelity, no love, no mercy." [7]

There is a *whole bunch* of other stuff on Paul's list, and it all comes *after* gay and lesbian sex. And a bunch of it is stuff I see in the church all the time. Greed? Gosh, that's pretty much an American pastime, and the church has done very little in the way of prophetic critique.[8] Gossip? That's not a problem at all in the church. Envy? I don't struggle with that one bit. Pride? For every gay Christian there are endless arrogant Christians. Self-promoting, insecure, bragging, robbing God of his due.

The church has been *so* vocal about homosexuality but has said so little about divorce, much less sex before marriage, both of which happen *all the time*. As I read it, the Scriptures' teaching on sex is unequivocal—all sex outside of marriage between a man and a woman is sin. Period. What's the point of rating which ones are the worst? Why not just repent and help each other move forward?

And because we haven't done a great job distinguishing between homosexual *attraction* and homosexual *sex*, we've pushed so many into hiding, heaping shame on them. But homosexual *attraction* is not sin, any more than heterosexual attraction is. It's what we do with it that matters. I'm attracted to women. That's not a sin. Lust is. And so is fantasy, and adultery, and so on.

The truth is that we all fall short. We all need Jesus. For those of you who live with same-sex attraction, you don't have to live in shame, any more than I do. You are loved. *Deeply* loved.

Myth 2: I'm straight, and you're gay

Another myth is that your sexuality is the most important thing about you. Labels like "gay" or "lesbian" or "bisexual" or "transgender" or "straight" are identity statements. It's a way of saying, "This is who I am." But to God, your sexuality does not define you. Rather, *God* defines you.

The Scriptures open by saying you are made in God's image. Because of that you have intrinsic value, worth, and dignity.

Later in the New Testament, followers of Jesus are called by a laundry list of identity statements — "holy," "blameless," "chosen," "sons and daughters," "brothers and sisters," etc. — and not one of them has to do with sexual orientation.

At the core of who we are, I'm not "straight" and you're not "gay." We are both *human*. We both bear God's image. Some of us are male, while others are female, but our identity is rooted in Jesus.

The problem is that we're all born bent. With a heart posture that is turned away from what is right and toward what is wrong. This is true of every human being on earth.

A while back, Rick Warren was interviewed by Ann Curry for *Dateline NBC*.[9] She was grilling him with provocative questions about his view on homosexuality. At one point she asked him what would happen if scientists found a gay gene, proving homosexuality was "natural." Would he change his position that gay sex is sin?

He said, "No."

She was shocked, but Warren went on to explain. "Just because something seems natural doesn't mean it's best for you or society." Then he said something profound. He said, "I'm naturally inclined to have sex with every beautiful woman I see. That doesn't mean it's the right thing to do."

In that moment, he was speaking for all straight men on the planet. At least, all the honest ones. That's embarrassing to admit, but it's true. I feel the same way at times. But that desire does not define me. It's not *who I am*. In fact, at times, I fight that desire with every cell in my body, because I know it's not the fully human way to live.

Gay sex isn't something you *are*, like black or female. It's something you *do* with your body. That's why a lot of my friends in the African-American community are so turned off when gay rights activists compare their struggle to the civil rights movement of the 1960s. It's not the same thing. My daughter, Sunday, is black.[10] She doesn't wake up in the morning and decide if she wants to be black or white that day. And while it's true that we don't have a choice in our orientation (although some of us do), we *all* have a choice in how we express our sexuality.

We need to do away with the labels of heterosexual and homosexual. There are just three labels in God's vision: human, male, and female. I would argue that it's all we need.[11]

Myth 3: The church isn't a safe place

One lie that my community is working hard to debunk is that the church isn't a safe place for people who are gay. That we're a bunch of mean, angry fundamentalists who picket military funerals in our spare time and teach our children that "God hates fags."

That's just not true. I have been around the church for my entire life, and I know followers of Jesus from all over the world and from across every spectrum. The overwhelming majority are kind, magnanimous, warm, loving people. They just don't get the airplay that mean people do. They don't make the news. But they are the norm.

The church is a family, and we want you to be a part of it. *Whoever you are.*

There are a growing number of gay people in our church. By "gay," I mean men and women who are attracted to members of the same sex but are fighting to stay pure and live the way of Jesus. I've heard story after story of how they have found a new family in the church. Fathers and mothers and brothers and sisters to wrestle with, pray with, cry with, repent with, and hope with. When a church is even close to what it's supposed to be, it's really something.

Just last week, I had a great talk with a girl named Sarah.[12] She spent years as a lesbian, before following Jesus. She was telling me how hard it is to be honest about her struggles in the church. How scared she is of what people will think. How awkward the conversations can be. But she was also telling me how she's found a family. And how her honesty is catalyzing honesty in others.

Not everybody in our church is on the same page. There are also a number of gay people who aren't convinced about what we believe, but they're sorting it through and not giving up on Jesus.

Wherever you're at, you're invited to the family of God. The church is a kaleidoscope of every age, every ethnicity, every walk of life, and every sexual orientation. As far as I can tell, there are only two common denominators: we're all screwed up, and we're all being put back together by Jesus.

Myth 4: Repressing your sexual desires is oppressive

A growing myth among both gay and straight people is that you have to follow your sexual desires in order to live free.

We live in the wake of the sexual revolution of the '60s, when our parents were running around naked at Woodstock.[13] That "revolution" created an ethos in the American psyche that says freedom and fulfillment are found in sexual self-expression. More than any other generation in American history, we're looking to sex for life.[14] That's why anything that curbs our sexual desires is seen as oppressive. To deny your feelings, your desires, your urges, is seen as denying *who you are*.

We think this way about all desires, not just sexual desires. Trust me, I get how complex this is for people. Homosexuality is way more than a desire for sex. It's a desire for friendship and intimacy, family and children, to grow old with someone you love. These are not bad desires — these are *human* desires. And it feels so cruel to say that if you're gay, you can't act on them.

But follow that logic all the way through. I'm a married man with three children. What if I were to "fall out of" love with my wife? We married young. We're very different. We have to work hard to keep our marriage healthy. What if it just gets to me at some point? And what if, around that same time, I fall in love with another woman? And what if those desires and urges I have for a life with her are real and authentic? What should I do? Give in to them, or deny them?

Even in the cultural milieu we live in, most people would say I should not act on those feelings, no matter how real they are. I should stay faithful to my wife and family. I should keep the vow I made all those years ago. And I should wrestle and struggle and fight to get my marriage back to a healthy space.

They would be right.

If you have to follow your sexual desires in order to find freedom and fulfillment, then what does that say about Jesus? He never married or had sex, not with a woman or a man. He was single and celibate his entire life. And don't think, "Yeah, but he was God." True, but he was also human, and not half-human or sorta-human. The writer of *Hebrews* tells us he was "tempted in every way, just as we are — yet he did not sin."[15] When Jesus saw a beautiful woman (or man) pass by, he was *just* as tempted to turn around and lust after her as I am. But unlike me, he never did. Not once.

And Jesus was anything but "oppressed." He was the freest human being to ever live.

Our wants are not the same thing as our needs. We don't *have* to follow our desires to live a fully human life. We just have to follow Jesus. Underneath all our desires and wants and needs and all the layers of identity and meaning is an image bearer created to live in relationship to God.

Myth 5: The Bible doesn't really teach that gay sex is a sin

This myth comes from a growing segment of the church. There are many good, sincere people who don't want to give up faith in Jesus to be gay. Faced with two options, Jesus or homosexuality, they're searching for an option C, but in doing so, they are reinterpreting the Scriptures to line up with culture.

Some people argue that the Bible's teaching on sexuality was *cultural*, just like head coverings or the holy kiss. It was written a long time ago, and we've since evolved to a much more progressive place.

The problem is that homosexuality *was* a part of the culture in the first century. And Greco-Roman culture was far more deviant than ours. Pederasty (older men having sex with adolescent boys) was widespread all over ancient Greece. Adultery was expected for Roman men. Incest was anything but rare. And, as Paul begins to write Romans 1, gay sex was a growing part of his world.[16]

We have pottery shards from around the time of Paul with carvings of two naked men staring into each other's eyes and holding each other's genitalia. Contrary to what I hear all the time, gay marriage is not a new idea.[17]

Caesar Nero, who was emperor right around the time Paul wrote *Romans*, was married to a twelve-year-old boy named Sporus. He made him dress in women's clothes and called him "lady." This, of course, was *after* he had already married a woman named Statilia Messalina *and* a man named Pythagoras. At that wedding, Nero played the wife. No president could get away with that kind of family life today.[18]

And it's to *that* world that the Scriptures, from cover to cover, call gay sex a sin.

Others argue that whatever the Bible is talking about, it's not the same thing as homosexuality in today's world. They interpret Paul's language to mean prostitution or promiscuity or pederasty, which most gay people would agree is wrong. They argue that as long as a couple is faithful to each other for life, gender doesn't matter.

The problem is that even if you could reinterpret all nine or ten passages in the Scriptures on homosexuality — and I don't think you can — you are still left with the narrative arc of the Bible, from *Genesis* to *Revelation*, that holds up God's vision of marriage as between a man and a woman. And Jesus was right in line with this vision. To Jesus, God's heart for marriage and sexuality, from the beginning, was a man and a woman.

Please don't take my word for it. Go read, study, probe, dig, argue — do your homework.[19] But I will tell you, I've read every argument I can find and have yet to find one that I think holds water.

Myth 6: Come to Jesus, and he'll make you straight

Sometimes, when the message of Jesus is presented, it sounds like, "Come to Jesus, and he'll fix you." As if all your problems and issues will go away the second you say yes. It's a cheap trick, really. Jesus is anything but easy.

It is true that Jesus can, and often does, change people dramatically. Even in sexual orientation. My friend Jason was attracted to men from childhood. He spent years in the gay and lesbian community. But ever since coming to faith in Jesus, God has been resculpting him into the man he intended. Jason is now married with three kids.[20]

I think of that line in *1 Corinthians*—"Do not be deceived: Neither the sexually immoral nor idolaters nor adulterers nor men who have sex with men nor thieves nor the greedy nor drunkards nor slanderers nor swindlers will inherit the kingdom of God. *And that is what some of you were.* But you were washed, you were sanctified, you were justified in the name of the Lord Jesus Christ and by the Spirit of our God."[21]

"That is what some of you were." Not *are*—*were*.

Entrance into the kingdom of God makes the impossible possible. The unthinkable thinkable.

But that's not always the case. If you follow Jesus, you may find your sexual preference start to change and revert to what God intended, *or* you may struggle to curb your sexual desires for the rest of your life.[22] I know men and women like this who have chosen celibacy to follow Jesus. It's not easy for them, but they are thriving.

You may never get married. You may live single for a long time. This isn't just true of sexual preference. A lot of people have to fight the temptation to alcohol or porn or gossip or worry for decades, but they make it through. In fact, they live rich, meaningful lives.

You may struggle, but you can struggle *well.*

Put down the myths, pick up the cross

The mantra of a post-1960s world is, "Express yourself. Follow your desires. Throw off the anchor of tradition. It's oppressive. Let the winds carry you to adventure. Be free. Be unique. Be yourself."

But the calling of the Rabbi from Nazareth is so very different. Jesus said, "Whoever wants to be my disciple must deny them-selves and take up their cross and follow me. For whoever wants to save their life will lose it, but whoever loses their life for me and for the gospel will save it."[23]

Whoever you are — gay, lesbian, bisexual, transgender, straight, or any other category we come up with — the invitation of Jesus is to deny yourself, take up your cross, and follow him.

In Jesus' day, the cross wasn't a religious cliché. It was a violent, barbaric symbol of death. It was an instrument of torture. Jesus is saying we all have stuff we have to "deny." We have to die to certain things if we want to follow him.

I know it sounds cruel for God to tell you that you can't be gay. But in a sense, what the Creator is asking of you isn't different from what he's asking of all of us.

Of the unmarried woman in her late thirties who wants so badly to be married but nobody has ever asked her.

Of the married man living with what the philosopher Thoreau called a "quiet desperation" in his marriage.

Of the married woman who was abused as a child and can't enjoy sex with her husband. It's painful — for her body and her soul.

Of all single people who want to have sex more than anything but know and believe and trust that the venue for sexuality is marriage. And so they wait.

In a sense, we all live with unfulfilled desires. That's not to downplay the struggle of our brothers and sisters who live with same-sex attraction. Rather, it's to stand in solidarity with you. We all have desires we can't act on. Evil desires, but also good desires, like a Jesus follower's desire to replace homosexual desires with heterosexual ones.

We live at the intersection of two worlds, waiting for what Paul called "the redemption of our bodies."[24]

That is the hope of the gospel. Nothing less than resurrection. There is coming a day when you will step into a world where the chaos and entropy of the fall are undone, and you will live forever in a body that is remade through a cosmic act of God. You will be free from any and all desires outside of God's vision. If you're gay now, you won't be then. If your marriage is broken now, it won't be then. If you're single now and sad about it, on that day you will be lonely for the last time.

Whatever your struggle is *now*, it will be worth it *then*.

Today, know that Jesus is with those of you who follow him. He knows what you're feeling. Really. He was tempted just like you, and his Spirit is inside you, ready to help you live his way.

And when that day comes, you want to look into Jesus' eyes and hear him say ...

"Well done.

You were good.

You were faithful.

You were my servant.

Enter into my joy." [25]

Epilogue

Let's cut the guy a little slack.

After all, he's had a rough life—it's almost like he was set up from birth. For starters, his twin brother, Esau, makes it out of the womb first. Being the firstborn is a huge deal in the ancient world, and Jacob *just* misses it. Maybe that's why he comes out of the womb seconds later with his hand wrapped around Esau's leg. From day one he's scraping to get ahead.

And then, of all the lousy things you can do to your child, his parents name him *Yaakov* in Hebrew, which means "heel grasper"—a Hebrew idiom for a deceiver, a liar.[1]

Thanks a ton, Mom and Dad.

And Jacob lives up to his name. His story is one lie after another. He deceives his older brother, Esau, to get the birthright of the first-born. He deceives his father, Isaac, to get the blessing. He deceives his uncle, Laban, to get the best flocks of sheep.

So he's always looking over his shoulder, trying to outrun each lie, but it doesn't work. Finally, *he* is deceived. The tables turn. The con artist gets played. It's as if the narrator of *Genesis* is saying, "What goes around comes around."[2]

And where does the heel grasper get deceived? In love.

Jacob is sent away from Canaan by his parents. Mostly to get away from his brother, who was going to kill him — literally. Ah, sibling rivalry. But also to find a wife in his native land, just like his father Isaac. He comes to the same town and to the same well where the servant had found his mother, Rebekah, decades before. And there he sees her. Rachel. The first thing the author of *Genesis* tells us is, "When Jacob saw Rachel daughter of his uncle Laban, and Laban's sheep, he went over and rolled the stone away from the mouth of the well and watered his uncle's sheep. Then Jacob kissed Rachel and began to weep aloud."[3]

That's the closest thing we get in the Scriptures to love at first sight. In Jacob's world, it was the woman's job to water the sheep, but Jacob is smitten at first sight.

A few paragraphs later, the text reads, "Now Laban had two daughters; the name of the older was Leah, and the name of the younger was Rachel. Leah had weak eyes, but Rachel had a lovely figure and was beautiful. Jacob was in love with Rachel ..."[4]

Sounds like a cheap novel, doesn't it? One man, two sisters ... Leah had "weak eyes." That's a Hebrew euphemism meaning "unattractive." In the ancient Near East, the majority of women were veiled. All a man could see was her eyes. If she had "bright eyes," that was a way of saying she was beautiful all over, but if she had "weak eyes," that was a gracious way of saying she was ugly.

But her younger sister, Rachel, "had a lovely figure and was beautiful." And so for obvious reasons, the next line reads, "Jacob was in love with Rachel."

There it is — the language we hear all the time. *In love.*

Most of the love stories in the Bible happen after marriage, because arranged marriage was the norm. But this one happens *before* the wedding. It's one of the few that bears any resemblance to what we think of as romantic love.[5] It has the two ingredients we all crave — sexual chemistry and deep feelings of affection. She "had a lovely figure," and Jacob was "in love."

Ironically, the story is a disaster.

Jacob wants to marry Rachel so badly that he offers to work for Laban for seven years in exchange for marriage. He knows his future father-in-law expects him to pay a bride-price, but Jacob is running for his life. He doesn't have a penny to his name. But Laban says yes, and Jacob gets to work. For seven years he is Laban's lackey — mucking out sheep pens, driving off wild animals, sleeping outside in the cold. But he's up for it. We read, "Jacob served seven years to get Rachel, but they seemed like only a few days to him because of his love for her." It sounds so romantic!

Finally Jacob says, "Give me my wife. My time is completed, and I want to make love to her."

At least he's honest, I'll give him that. In essence he's saying, "Father-in-law-to-be, I worked my butt off for you, but now I want to have sex with your daughter. Give her to me. Like, now."

Laban has no choice but to say yes, so he calls together the village for a wedding feast. Everybody's there. Family, friends, neighbors — and they all party hard into the night. Jacob is thinking, "Finally, after *seven years of waiting* I get her. Rachel."

He goes into the tent, and there she is, in the dark, ready, and the camera pans to the ceiling ...

But the next day Jacob is in for a surprise. The text reads, "When morning came, there was Leah!"

It isn't Rachel!

Jacob wakes up in a snit and barges into Laban's tent. "What is this you have done to me? I served you for Rachel, didn't I? Why have you deceived me?"

The deceiver is deceived. Remember, this is 2000 BC. There's no mood lighting in the tent at night. And women wear a veil during the day. It's not until the sun comes up that Jacob sees he's been duped. And then there's that line ...

When morning came, there was Leah!

Life's like that, isn't it?

You work and sweat and wait and wonder and hope and anticipate, and then, *finally*, you make it. You arrive. And it's incredible for a night, but then you wake up in the morning, and it's Leah.

It's weak eyes.

It's a letdown. A disappointment. Not what you had hoped for.

Life is full of letdowns. The human experience is anything but ideal.

Whatever "it" is for you — college, graduation, a job, travel, an experience, success, fame, money, beauty — trust me, it's Leah. It can't live up to your expectations.

Guess what? The same is true of marriage. Marriage will let you down. Don't get me wrong, marriage is *incredible*. But it's not paradise.

I love Paul's one-sentence description of marriage — "Those who marry will face many troubles in this life." Take one broken person with pain and regret and baggage and idealism and an odd uncle. Now add another broken person with problems and issues and unrealistic expectations and an overbearing mother-in-law. Friends, *that does not equal bliss*!

In fact, the math adds up to twice as much crap.

We usually make one of two mistakes in love — and this applies to life as well. Some of us under-desire marriage (or a career or success or a dream), and so we settle. And we're damned to mediocrity. The torture of the mundane. We never really *live*. We're too scared or too cynical or just too tired to actually dream. We are the "realists," but we all know that's just code for pessimists in denial. We're rarely let down because we aren't brave enough to risk.

The rest of us over-desire marriage (or college or graduation or whatever). We risk and step out and go for it. We're fueled by the audacious sense that anything is possible. We are the idealists, the entrepreneurs, the dreamers, the artists, the explorers, and the lovers. We grow up dreaming about love. We put so much pressure on marriage, sex, and romance to fulfill us that it ends up creating a weird sort of pathology in our life. We might marry multiple times, as if searching for something more — and believing, against all the odds, that *this time it will be different*, this time we'll find what was lacking the first time around.

Wherever we fall in the spectrum, it's only a matter of time until we wake up one morning — and we're lying next to Leah.

But here's why I've been telling you the story of Jacob. There's an upside. God is in the letdowns. He's in the disappointments.

In the end, Jacob does marry Rachel. He has to work another seven years, but he gets his love. So now he's married to *both* sisters. To say the family was dysfunctional would be generous. Leah knows she's second-string. Jacob knows his father-in-law screwed him over. And Rachel? Over the years, Rachel turns out to be a problem. Her character falls short of her beauty. She lies, steals, and worships other gods, and for years she is barren. In the ancient world, that was a crushing blow to a woman's name. Sons were everything — labor force, militia, retirement plan. Thankfully, she eventually has two sons, which is a narrow save.

What about Leah? Weak eyes? She has *eight sons*! And one of her sons was named Judah, and from his tribe comes the long line of Israelite kings — David, Solomon, Hezekiah, Josiah ... and hundreds of years later, one born in a cave in Bethlehem — the Messiah, Jesus.

God isn't just in the letdowns of life. He *uses* the letdowns of life. The dreams and accomplishments and relationships and marriages that don't measure up. Even in a screwed-up family with a polygamous marriage that was anything but what God intended in the garden, God was at work. God uses our sin. He uses our mistakes. Our misjudgments. Our bad decisions.

Because it's about marriage, but it's not about marriage at all.

There's this story in the Gospels where Jesus is fielding a barrage of questions from the religious leaders in Jerusalem. They're jealous of Jesus' growing following and scared to death of his teaching. If he's right, everything is about to change.

One day, "the Sadducees, who say there is no resurrection, came to him with a question."[6] The Sadducees were a group of aristocratic, well-off, educated religious leaders in Jerusalem. Unlike the Pharisees, they only believed that the books of Moses (*Genesis* through *Deuteronomy*) were inspired by God. The rest of the Scriptures — what you and I call the Old Testament — they rejected. And because most of the passages about resurrection are in the Prophets, they didn't buy in to the idea. They believed that this life is it. After it's over, there's nothing but the grave. No resurrection, no world to come, no Eden redone. You live, you die, and you're done. The best you can do is to live well for a few short decades.

Sound familiar?

The Sadducees ask Jesus about an obscure text in the Torah where "Moses wrote for us that if a man's brother dies and leaves a wife but no children, the man must marry the widow and raise up offspring for his brother." This shows you how differently they viewed marriage in the ancient world. It was a means to an end. And if you're a Sadducee and you don't buy the idea of a resurrection, then your "offspring" are your future. The way you live on in the world.

So they test Jesus with this bizarre question — "Now there were seven brothers. The first one married and died without leaving any children. The second one married the widow, but he also died, leaving no child. It was the same with the third. In fact, none of the seven left any children. Last of all, the woman died too. At the resurrection whose wife will she be, since the seven were married to her?"[7]

You would think they would figure out something's up by about brother number four. This woman was seriously bad news.[8]

Jesus answers them with, "Are you not in error because you do not know the Scriptures or the power of God? When the dead rise, *they will neither marry nor be given in marriage*; they will be like the angels in heaven."[9]

To Jesus, marriage is a stopgap. A hold-me-over. A way to get by until what he called "the renewal of all things."[10] In the future, when the dead rise, and you and I stand in front of God and step into his remade world, there won't be any marriage. I have no doubt that my wife and I will know and love each other and hopefully spend time together, but we won't be the Comers anymore. My left ring finger will be bare.

This means that everything we've covered in this book — love, marriage, sex, relationships — it's all penultimate. At its best, it's a shadow, a glimpse of what's coming in the future.

Maybe that's why the Scriptures end with the wedding of heaven and earth. Have you ever read the last two chapters of the Bible and noticed all the Eden imagery?

"On each side of the river stood the tree of life ..."

"The leaves of the tree are for the healing of the nations ..."

"No longer will there be any curse ..."

"They will reign for ever and ever ..."[11]

This future world — the one that is now breaking in through Jesus and his followers and that one day will come in force — is like Eden, but it's something more, something even better. It's not just a garden — it's a gardenlike city. It's not just Adam and Eve — it's "persons from every tribe and language and people and nation."[12] And it's not just marriage between a man and a woman — it's all of humanity united in relationship with God *forever*. John writes, "They will be his people, and God himself will be with them and be their God."[13]

Are you single? Married?

Are you lonely? In love?

Are you hurting? Hopeful?

Wherever you're coming from, here's what you can know with certainty. *This life is a gift.*

Love, marriage, sex, even singleness — this whole thing was created by God. It's good, and it's for you to enjoy. I hope and pray you do that well. Live the way God made you to live. The way of Jesus — what one writer called "the life that is truly life."[14]

But know this as well. Nothing in this world can fill the gaping void left in your heart by our departure from Eden. Not the best marriage, the best sex, the best romance — nothing. All that stuff is incredible, but it's not God.

The letdowns will come.

And when they do, remind yourself that this life, in its best moments, is nothing more than a signpost pointing forward to the age to come.

The day when "there will be no more death or mourning or crying or pain."[15] When "sorrow and sighing will flee away."[16] And when we will be *with God*, just like we were supposed to be in the beginning.

My guess is that's why the closing paragraph of the Bible is a prayer that's wrapped up in wedding imagery. A Jewish bride never knew the exact day of her wedding. She just knew her lover was coming soon, "at an hour [she] is not aware of."[17] So she would live every day with one eye fixed on the window … waiting.

That's actually a pretty good way to live *all of life*.

"The Spirit and the bride say, 'Come!'"[18]

Proverbs 8

Does not wisdom call out? Does not understanding raise her voice? At the highest point along the way, where the paths meet, she takes her stand; beside the gate leading into the city, at the entrance, she cries aloud: "To you, O people, I call out; I raise my voice to all mankind. You who are simple, gain prudence; you who are foolish, set your hearts on it. Listen, for I have trustworthy things to say; I open my lips to speak what is right. My mouth speaks what is true, for my lips detest wickedness. All the words of my mouth are just; none of them is crooked or perverse. To the discerning all of them are right; they are upright to those who have found knowledge. Choose my instruction instead of silver, knowledge rather than choice gold, for wisdom is more precious than rubies, and nothing you desire can compare with her. I, wisdom, dwell together with prudence; I possess knowledge and discretion. To fear the LORD is to hate evil; I hate pride and arrogance, evil behavior and perverse speech. Counsel and sound judgment are mine; I have insight, I have power. By me kings reign and rulers issue decrees that are just; by me princes govern, and nobles — all who rule on earth. I love those who love me, and those who seek me find me. With me are riches and honor, enduring wealth and prosperity. My fruit is better than fine gold; what I yield surpasses choice silver. I walk in the way of righteousness, along the paths of justice, bestowing a rich inheritance on those who love me and making their treasuries full. The LORD brought me forth as the first of his works, before his deeds of old; I was formed long ages ago, at the very beginning, when the world came to be. When there were no watery depths, I was given birth, when there were no springs overflowing with water; before the mountains were settled in place, before the hills, I was given birth, before he made the world or its fields or any of the dust of the earth. I was there when he set the heavens in place, when he marked out the horizon on the face of the deep, when he established the clouds above and fixed securely the fountains of the deep, when he gave the sea its boundary so the waters would not overstep his command, and when he marked out the foundations of the earth. Then I was constantly at his side. I was filled with delight day after day, rejoicing always in his presence, rejoicing in his whole world and delighting in mankind. Now then, my children, listen to me; blessed are those who keep my ways. Listen to my instruction and be wise; do not disregard it. Blessed are those who listen to me, watching daily at my doors, waiting at my doorway. For those who find me find life and receive favor from the LORD. But those who fail to find me harm themselves; all who hate me love death."

Q and A

Before *Loveology* was a book, it was an event. A while back, we crammed two thousand twentysomethings into an empty warehouse in the Pearl District of Portland. By "warehouse" I mean a concrete box. No heaters. No bathrooms. No windows. Just mounds of amorous young ones, sitting in 360 degrees around a four-by-eight stage, and eating up a theology of love, marriage, sex, and all the rest.

We ended each night with a live Q and A that stretched past midnight. It was by far the highlight of the event. There's nothing like raw, uncut conversation to pull you off the edge of your seat.

So this time around I enlisted the help of my wife, Tammy, and Dr. Gerry Breshears to give it another go. Tam is by far the wisest person I've ever met, and she has that prophetic kind of wisdom that cuts to the heart. Dr. Breshears is a professor, writer, and head of the theology department at Western Seminary in Portland, but he's no detached, aloof academic. He's rooted in the church and spends tons of his "free time" counseling. All that makes him the Klondike for stuff like this.

The following questions are 100 percent real. They're either from the event or have been asked by our church folks in a recent follow-up Q and A. Not one of these was made up by myself or an editor. Feel free to peruse, skip, skim, or read every line. I hope it's helpful.

Questions on love

Question: People always told me about the dangers of physical ties in a dating relationship, but no one warned me about the emotional dangers. What are some good boundaries or rules to help guard my heart emotionally in relationships before marriage?

John Mark: One word — *pace*. A relationship needs to move at the right speed. So many couples dive in headfirst. This is romantic, but potentially dangerous. Slow down. Take your time. Fools rush in. Turn the volume down from 11. Life is long. No need to leap ahead.

And remember that the whole point of dating is to figure out if this is somebody you want to marry, not to emotionally connect with somebody you barely know. Don't lay your whole life out on the table on your first date. Get to know each other. Build a friendship. Don't ever forget that the foundation of every healthy relationship is friendship.

But at the same time, no matter how you come at it, love is a risk. But it's a risk worth taking. If you guard yourself too much, you'll never get to experience love.

Tammy: I see people all the time (usually women) who are so emotionally guarded that they won't let anybody in, and because of that, they end up alone. You can't live that way.

To be honest, there is fallout when *any* relationship ends, no matter what pace you move at. Humans are emotional creatures. We don't mean to sound trite, but if your heart gets broken, God can put it back together.

Question: What's the difference between lust and attraction? When is it holy and pure to have strong feelings for a person you're dating, while not turning those feelings into lustful sin?

John Mark: As I see it, lust is when we look at a woman (or a man) *for the purpose* of desire. Dallas Willard says it's when "we desire to desire."[1] It's when we indulge, play with, mull on, tantalize, fantasize, and play with desire. When a woman or a man is an object for our imagination to play out sexual fantasy. Lust is selfish. It starts and ends with *me*.

Attraction, on the other hand, is when we find a woman or a man beautiful because we see them as created in God's image. There's absolutely nothing wrong with enjoying the beauty of another human being, but, for men in particular, it's a slippery slope from "enjoying the beauty" to lust.

In his talk on the hill, Jesus calls his followers to a life free from lust.[2] It can be achieved through the empowering presence of Jesus' Spirit.

Question: Why is fantasizing bad?

John Mark: Because *nobody* can live up to the ideal in your mind. Whether it's porn, voyeurism, imagining the girl in your apartment complex naked, romance novels, chick flicks, or thinking about life married to another person — no human being can actually live up to that. Fantasy sets us up to be disappointed, and disappointing.

Fantasizing before marriage primes you for disillusionment, and once you're married, it can set the stage for adultery.

Tammy: I know we usually refer to guys when it comes to fantasizing, but women, be careful how you think too. If you're looking for Edward Cullen to sweep you off your feet, you'll not only miss out on reality, but you could well miss out on a great guy who would love you well. Romance novels and films set you up for disillusionment. And it isn't fair to your boyfriend or husband. *Edward Cullen isn't real.* In fact, in real life he has relationship issues, as do 99 percent of the celebrities we dream about. Your mind is your greatest asset when it comes to sex. But it can also be your biggest enemy. How you think and what you think about will determine how happy you are in your marriage.

Gerry: You are what you think. GIGO. That's why Paul tells us to think about what is pure and lovely.[3] Then you can enjoy the wonderful trust that you will have between husband and wife.

Question: Is it wrong to be with someone who has faith but isn't sure what they believe in?

John Mark: YES! Faith in what? It's not generic spirituality that glues a relationship together. It's Jesus.

If by "isn't sure what they believe in" you mean "isn't sure about how to interpret the book of *Revelation*" or something like that, sure. Stuff like that is healthy. But I'm assuming you mean isn't sure about Jesus versus Buddha versus Allah versus "spirituality." If so, slam on the brakes.

Tammy: It's so important to be on the same page with Jesus when you get married. It sets the foundation for your life together. If and when you have children, it's one of those things that can be really divisive and painful.

Gerry: Before you get emotionally involved, spend time in an exploratory Bible study and learn about Jesus. You don't have to stop the relationship just because of vague faith. Build your Jesus-heart. The learning together can be a wonderful bonding time if the direction is into Jesus.

Questions on marriage

Question: What if you love the Lord and you love each other, and you both have a mission, but they aren't similar missions? Say one person is working to teach children computer coding, and the other is passionate about spreading the gospel through performance comedy. Is this a problem?

John Mark: Well, it depends. Are your missions contradictory or complementary? If they are contradictory, then, yes, that's a problem, and a serious one at that. If one of you can't do what *you know* God has called you to do, then you should break up. The whole point of marriage is to partner together for God's calling on your life. You should marry someone who will at least *help* you do that, not hold you back.

But if your missions are complementary, then you're in good shape. Don't confuse your calling with your job or your passion. Often they are one and the same, but not always. One of you might be all about computer coding, and the other performance comedy (I'm assuming this is hypothetical!), but your calling is to live out the gospel in your city.

Tammy: The trick is to find the common ground. What are you *both* called to do? Where do your missions overlap? And women, can you get behind his vision? When it comes to mission, one heart is essential. Having differing roles is okay, even good, but the point is to garden together. Can you partner with him? If not, you may need to rethink either your calling or your relationship.

Gerry: I just finished counseling a couple who was wrestling with divergent callings. He felt called to teach science in Muslim-dominated North Africa, but she felt called to be a mom and raise her kids in a safe environment (after growing up as a missionary kid in constant danger). They were able to think creatively about the future. He landed a job in the Persian Gulf, which is both Muslim and safe, and they were able to make it work.

That's what you're looking for. An option C. If you can't find it, don't sacrifice your calling for a spouse.

Question: Is it okay to discuss with someone you're planning to marry what you want your sex life to be like? As in, is it okay to make sure the two of you are on the same page as far as sex goes?

Tammy: Yes, of course. Just do it at the right time.

Early in the relationship all you should talk about is sexual values. How you think about sex is really important. Do you view it as good and fun (in the context of marriage)? Or do you think of it as dirty? A healthy perspective on sex will set you up for a fun life together once you're hitched. So I would say talk about it for sure, just not in great detail. Then, after you get engaged, talk in depth about your coming sexual relationship. Just don't act it out. That's what the honeymoon is for.

Gerry: When you go through premarital counseling — hopefully with a Jesus-loving counselor, pastor, or mentor — they will walk you through this process. It's fun stuff.

Question: What's the Bible's take on practicing safe sex?

John Mark: Um, it's called marriage.

Just to clarify, any and all sex outside of marriage between a man and a woman is sin. There is no such thing as safe sex outside of marriage. You may not get pregnant if you use a condom or birth control, but you tear *echad*, and nobody is immune to that pain.

Gerry: It is important to understand that biblically, sex is a whole-person bonding activity between a husband and wife to increase and deepen marital friendship and intimacy. The American view that it is a recreational activity between consenting adults is totally unacceptable. Really sacrilege — turning God's beautiful gift into a commodity.

Question: Is oral sex between my wife and me considered a sin?

John Mark: Heck no. Where in the world would you get that idea? Definitely not from the Scriptures. Some scholars think Song of Songs 2v3 is an allusion to oral sex — "Like an apple tree among the trees of the forest is my beloved among the young men. I delight to sit in his shade, *and his fruit is sweet to my taste.*" Whether or not that's what the poet is saying, God created sex, and it's very good. All of it.

Tammy: Biblically, you are totally safe. Guys, I would just encourage you to ask her before you go all crazy. She may need to ease into your idea, and it will help if you tell her that you're excited about making love to her in that way. Most women hesitate with oral sex because they think it's bad, or it kinda weirds them out. But if you can explain to her that your heart is for oneness, then it could be a great way to serve each other.

Question: All types of sex are fair once you're married, right? Even kinky acts? As long as it's not going outside of marriage?

John Mark + Tammy: We would say *anything goes* as long as it's (1) in line with the heart and character of God — who is compassionate, gracious, slow to anger, abounding in love and faithfulness, forgiving, etc.[4] — and (2) mutually pleasurable. Remember that sex is about giving, not getting. It's a way to serve your spouse, not act out twisted stuff you see online.

Gerry: The word "kinky" makes me think of stuff like porn and bondage paraphernalia, which is not compatible with God's heart at all. But other than the dark stuff, have fun!

Question: I was sexually abused as a little girl for many years. Is it possible for me to have a normal intimate relationship after I get married?

John Mark: Yes. Absolutely. You can have incredible sex, but it may take time. Your view of sex is probably warped and contorted because of the abuse. Open up your life to Jesus, and let him start his healing work. He can reframe how you view sex. Ask him to help you view sex as a good thing and help you enjoy sex as a gift and as a way to deep intimacy with your spouse.

Tammy: Once you get married, sex can actually be a part of your healing. Your future husband needs to learn how to love you toward sexual healing. It's not just your job to figure it out. This is something you should work on together. He needs to create a safe place for you to be vulnerable and honest. To listen and enter into your pain without trying to "fix" you. Your job is to risk and trust. Talk about how you're feeling. Open up. Tell the truth. And watch the Spirit of Jesus work in your relationship.

Gerry: Sexual abuse can wound the whole person. A physician may be necessary for healing your body. Your wounded spirit often needs the expert healing of a counselor. This is best when the counselor is a Jesus lover who can help with the spiritual dimension along with the emotional trauma. First John 1v9 tells us to confess our sins, and God "is faithful and just and will forgive us our sins and purify us from all unrighteousness." Sin includes things done by us, to us, and in our presence that defile us. When we talk about what happened with Jesus, he not only forgives sins we have done but cleanses the defilement of things done to us. The feeling "I'm gross, dirty" that many abuse survivors feel can be sent away as the scapegoat was on the Day of Atonement.[5]

Question: My parents are pressuring my younger sister to get married because she is living in sin. Are my parents addressing the right issue?

Tammy: Not necessarily. Two wrongs don't make a right. Just because she's living in sin, or even if she were to get pregnant, that doesn't mean the right thing to do is get married. The first and most important question is whether or not they are a good fit.

Some friends of ours had a similar situation. They were young when she got pregnant. In an attempt to "make it right," they got married, but a decade and three kids later, they were still having the same issues. She cheated on him. They divorced. And the kids paid the price for it. Usually if you start out a marriage on the wrong foot, it's hard to press the reset button years later when you realize you were never a good fit to begin with.

Question: I was baptized after marriage, and my spouse is not religious. Many of my Christian friends don't believe we should stay together because we are "unequally yoked."

John Mark: You need to get new friends. No offense. You are getting *really* bad advice. In 1 Corinthians 7, Paul makes it crystal clear what you should do. Go read it right now. Essentially, he says that if your spouse is willing to stay with you, then you should stay in the marriage. Hopefully they will come to faith in Jesus because of watching you up close.

Tammy: A good friend of mine is starting to follow Jesus, but her husband is an atheist. As hard as that is, they have a great marriage and are making it work. And we're all praying for her husband.

God's heart is to see your husband walk with him. Pray for him. Love him. Be loyal to him. Your friends are totally off here.

Question: What are your thoughts on remarriage after divorce?

Gerry: This is a really hard one, as so many people, including young people, have been divorced. More and more, we talk with people in their mid-twenties who are already divorced and dating again.

Answering this question well is beyond the scope of this Q and A section, but I have a message on it ("Testing Jesus on Divorce") that you can download from "Gerry's Sermon Recordings," http://sdrv.ms/17b2wnT (accessed September 4, 2013).

Also, make sure you understand the various readings of Jesus' teachings on divorce. For an overview of each, read the book edited by Mark Strauss titled *Remarriage after Divorce in Today's Church: 3 Views* (Grand Rapids: Zondervan, 2006), with contributions by Gordon Wenham, William Heth, and Craig Keener. Remember, the "best" answer is the one that makes the most sense of the Scriptures involved, not just the one you want to hear.

John Mark: That said, here's our short answer. Divorce is wrong. Period. Marriage is a covenant, not a contract. The idea of "biblical grounds for divorce" is a myth. That language isn't found anywhere in the Bible. Even in cases of adultery, which is gut-wrenching, God's heart is always *repentance and restoration*. Always! That's at the heart of the gospel. But there are times when a marriage dies. Divorce is the recognition that the marriage is no longer alive. Jesus gives adultery as an example of a marriage killer. Paul gives another one, abandonment, which makes me think Jesus' list isn't exhaustive.

Gerry: I could not agree more. It is tragic and sinful when a marriage dies or when people give up on a wounded marriage. Jesus' heart is always for both spouses to repent of sin, make things right, and start the long walk to healing. But marriages do die, and divorce is not the unforgivable sin.

John Mark: I agree. But remarriage is sticky. Jesus teaches, "Anyone who divorces his wife and marries another woman commits adultery against her. And if she divorces her husband and marries another man, she commits adultery."[6] We need to take this text seriously. Jesus is *the* authority.

There are two ways of reading the text. One is to say that if you remarry after divorce, you are committing the sin of adultery. That means if you are divorced, you're done. Singleness is a valid option for you. Jesus was single, and so was Paul. It's not a curse. You would be better off divorced and single than divorced and remarried. A number of sharp, intelligent scholars read the text that way.

The other reading is that Jesus is assuming the cast-off wife will remarry, and that's why he's calling it adultery, caused by the husband who divorced her. So the divorce itself *is* adultery. In the modern world, either spouse can end the marriage. But if you walk out on your spouse, technically, you are guilty of the sin of adultery. You need to repent (not make excuses) and ask God, your ex-spouse, his or her family, your friends, etc., to forgive you. If neither of you has remarried, you should seriously think and pray about remarriage to each other.

Tammy: This just happened in our church. A young couple divorced after a rocky marriage. He was promiscuous after the breakup, but then they were moved by the Spirit of Jesus to restart. They dated again and then remarried. They just had baby number one and are thriving. That story can be your story.

Gerry: If that's not an option, then we could see a scenario where a divorced disciple of Jesus remarried, but only if (1) a good deal of time has passed for healing and change so you can actually bless your next spouse, not just drag your crap into another marriage; (2) you have actually owned up to your sin in the divorce, repented, and made things right (not just paid lip service); (3) you've done business with your baggage, and you're sure you aren't going to make the same mistake twice; and (4) your future spouse is okay with the pain you will carry into your second marriage and is willing to work through it with you.

John Mark: I just sat with a guy last week after church. He divorced at the age of twenty-four of his own free will. Now he's twenty-seven, walking with Jesus again and wanting to date a girl in our church. Tammy has been spending a bunch of time with her, helping her sort this out. She's interested but wants to follow Jesus' teachings. Rather than just diving in, they wanted to get our advice. We had a great talk. I'm proud of them for wrestling with the issue and not just bounding forward.

This is a hard one, for sure. We lean toward the second reading, but with lots of trepidation. *Please* do your homework. Read up. Pray. Take the heart posture of Jesus — "Not what I will, but what you will." [7]

Questions on sex

Question: Is it lust to get aroused by doing something that isn't sex, like kissing?

John Mark: It's natural to get aroused by kissing or even by sight. Just looking at my wife in a summer dress does that for me, and we've been married for a decade. That's how God created our bodies to work.

Gerry: They key is, as soon as you get aroused, you need to stop — kissing, looking, cuddling, whatever. Better yet, know when you get aroused ahead of time, and avoid it. Remember *The Song* says three times, "Do not arouse or awaken love until it so desires."[8] Don't activate that part of your relationship until you can follow it all the way to the end.

Question: What does the Bible say about masturbation? I know a lot of girls who struggle with it, not just men. Is masturbation wrong? It's always treated as a taboo subject in the church.

John Mark: To be honest, there is no overt text on masturbation anywhere in the Bible. Some scholars think Jesus is alluding to it in the Sermon on the Mount. Right after talking about lust, he says, "If your right eye causes you to stumble, gouge it out ... And if your hand causes you stumble, cut it off and throw it away. It is better for you to lose one part of your body than for your whole body to go into hell."[9] That could be what Jesus is talking about, but we don't know for sure.

The fact is that masturbation is never specifically called out as sin anywhere in the Bible. *But lust is.* Jesus was crystal clear on that one: "I tell you that anyone who looks at a woman lustfully has already committed adultery with her in his heart."[10] Jesus takes lust really seriously, and so should we, no matter how trivial it is in culture. That said, the fact that masturbation isn't on any of the major sin lists in the New Testament means you should not define your walk with Jesus by whether or not you jacked off that day.[11]

Gerry: I think there is a place for a man to masturbate for sexual release, as long as his thoughts are on the release and he's not lusting. I don't recommend it, but for a sex-charged man with an extra high need for release, it's better than wet dreams, which are always lustful, or going crazy all the time. I see it as "the lesser of two evils."

John Mark: I see where Gerry is coming from, but I don't see how a man could masturbate without lusting. For me, that just sets a man up for temptation. Personally, I don't have the self-control to do that.

Tammy: As we're sitting in my living room writing this, I'm just smiling and feeling a little awkward. Seriously, for a woman there's no sexual release, so I think for us it's just lust.

Question: I had sex. What is the point of waiting for marriage now?

Gerry: Well, on the negative side, follow that line of reasoning all the way through. "I robbed a bank once, so what is the point of waiting until I get a job to do it again?" If something is wrong, it's *always* wrong.

But from the positive angle, if you've sinned but since repented and experienced God's grace and healing, then you want to carry that into your new marriage. Sex before marriage is very different from sex in marriage. It may be more exhilarating at first, but not nearly as good overall.

Question: If you wait until marriage for sex, then how will you know if you are sexually compatible with your partner?

Gerry: Sexual compatibility is basically a myth. The vast majority of compatibility is relational, not physical. For the few couples where there is a physical issue (such as he's a seven-foot linebacker and she's petite), you can usually find a way to make it work, but that is something you should think through before you get married.

Tammy: I see sex as an art form. One that you learn and practice. Sexual compatibility isn't something you "have" or "don't have." Over time, in marriage, you get better and better at giving your spouse pleasure in bed. You learn what they like. That's why sex in marriage is so much fun. It honestly gets *more* fun the longer you're married.

Question: Why would I wait for my honeymoon to have awkward and possibly disappointing honeymoon sex?

Tammy: For starters, the honeymoon does not need to be awkward or disappointing. Ours was a ton of fun. Set the stage well in dating, and it will make all the difference in the world. Read a few good books,[12] talk with a counselor, dialogue with each other, go into it ready, and you'll do great.

Honeymoon sex is a blast because you're discovering each other (ideally) for the first time and learning about each other in a whole new way. Months of buildup and anticipation all come together on your wedding day. It's not going to look like a scene from a James Bond movie, but that's okay. It's still a ton of fun. You get to learn together how to be "naked and unashamed," with God's full blessing. And you have your whole life to figure it out. Just focus on becoming one. The rest will take care of itself.

Gerry: So good, Tammy. The first time will be a learning experience, so the best thing is to do it with God's full blessing and help.

Question: Why is sex solely about performance in today's culture? Men expect women to act out what is viewed in porn, and we just can't live up to that expectation. Is there hope for men to change this performance-centered view of sex, or is this just going to get worse?

John Mark: Our guess is that culture will continue down the trajectory it's on — toward rampant pornographic sadism. Sadly, smut is one of the few things America exports well. More and more people will be warped in how they think about sex. The objectification of women, the sexualization of romance, and the proliferation of heartache will continue to multiply.

But any man or woman can change their view of sex. No damage is irreparable. The healing Spirit of Jesus can do wonders, literally.

Tammy: And to clarify, it's not just men. Men may have a performance-centered view of sex, but women often have a performance-centered view of *romance*. This is really intimidating for guys. No man can compete with a vegan vampire. We should respect men who are walking with Jesus and fighting to stay pure. Encourage them. They're not perfect, but they're fighting for it — that's saying something. Believe the best about them, and don't project your disapproval of culture on all men. Unless he gives you a reason not to trust him, encourage him in the fight. When you're married, the best way to do that is to have sex with him — a lot.

Question: Why did God make men so incredibly sexual? As a woman, it intimidates me how sex crazed men are today. Do they truly think about sex every hour of every day?

Gerry: No, men don't think about sex 24/7. That's a caricature from TV sitcoms, not from real life. And it's not what good men are like. For those men (and women) who *are* sex obsessed, God didn't make men that way. That is the by-product of sin.

John Mark: As a general rule (I'm not trying to stereotype here, just point out a pattern), men are more physically oriented in sexuality and women are more relationally oriented in sexuality, but that doesn't mean men are sex crazed.

Tammy: And women, don't forget, love "believes all things."[14] Always believe the best about the men in your life. Speak truth over them. They will become what you say they are.

Questions on romance

Question: Is it good to take a long time to become best friends before getting into a dating relationship?

Tammy: Depends on what you mean by a "long time." It's a smart idea to get to know each other as friends for a while before you start dating, or at least before you get serious. Friendship is at the heart of a healthy relationship. But I don't think there's a need to wait much longer than three months.

Gerry: Here's a good rule of thumb: three months of friendship (no touch), three to six months of dating (limited, nonarousing touch), one month to dialogue with family and friends to make a decision, and three months of engagement. All in all, about a year from first date to marriage. There's no one-size-fits-all relationship, but that's a good place to start.

John Mark: Yeah, that's a hard one. We dated for two years, and it was a year too long! But for others, I think Gerry's timeline might be a little too fast. A lot depends on your age and stage of life. The younger you are, the more time you should take to sort it out.

Question: When is the right time to tell the person I'm dating about my past sexual sin? How much detail do I go into? I want to be open and honest about my past, but I also don't want to let someone into that part of my life too soon.

Gerry: Timing is a hard one, but I would say it should be before your relationship gets serious and you start bonding emotionally. You want to learn about each other's pasts while you can still make a logical decision about whether or not to go forward.

As for how much detail, I think the more the better. I know it's hard to wade into all the stuff you regret, but it's not details that kill intimacy. It's secrets. There should be *no* secrets in marriage. None.

John Mark: I *so* agree.

Gerry: Often people say, "I don't want to hurt him or her," but the odds are, that's a lie. The reality is you don't want to talk about your sin because it's embarrassing. You're probably avoiding your own hurt. But talking about your sin (what the Scriptures call "confession") can be a powerful step forward in healing. It opens the door for forgiveness from God and from your spouse-to-be, breaking guilt and shame's hold on your life. And coming together to overcome your past can actually enrich intimacy in marriage. Brutal as it can be, this is a really good, healthy, freeing thing.

Question: Everyone tells us that "how far is too far?" is the wrong question to ask and that we should stay as far away from the line as possible. This is heartwarming but not very practical. Is it wrong to hug, kiss, or make out? What is the correct stance on physical relations in a dating relationship?

All three of us: Great question. Here's our advice ...

1. Don't do anything in private that you wouldn't do in public. That's a great rule of thumb. We would kiss in public but not make out. Hug, but not the ten-minute full-body-sway-with-back-massage kind of hug.

2. Don't cross the line from affection to arousal. The second you are aroused, stop.

3. Don't ever be alone together in a house or apartment. It's really hard to get pregnant with your roommate sitting on the couch next to you! A few people gave us this advice when we started dating, and honestly, if we hadn't done it, my guess is our seven-year-old would be thirteen right now. It was a pain. I lived in a house full of guys, and she lived with her parents. Whenever they left for anything, we had to step out. We spent a lot of time at coffee shops and parks. But it was a lifesaver.

4. Talk about "the line" together, early on in the relationship. I know it's awkward, but it's important. That way you can make a plan together and hold each other to your joint decision.

Question: How long should you wait to kiss?

Tammy: We waited until engagement to kiss on the lips, and we don't regret it at all. In fact, after we started kissing we *barely* made it to the wedding day. Once you open that door, it's really, really hard not to walk through it.

John Mark: I have actually never kissed another woman, and to be honest, kissing is the best part of my sexual relationship with

Tammy. If you're young and have that as an option, you should at least think about it. But if that's too harsh for you, our advice is to wait until the relationship gets serious. And remember that kissing should always be done apart from cuddling. Not on the couch all alone late at night, by candlelight, with Bon Iver playing in the background. You don't need to arouse or awaken that part of your relationship until marriage.

Question: What if you agree on not having sex before marriage, but the other person REALLY wants to spend the night just sleeping with you. Is that appropriate? Is it ever appropriate before marriage? Why or why not?

Tammy: No. I don't mean to sound harsh, but that's just stupid. Why would you do that? You're setting yourself up for temptation.

John Mark: I think of James — "Each person is tempted when they are dragged away by *their own evil desires* and enticed. Then, after desire has conceived, it gives birth to sin; and sin, when it is full-grown, gives birth to death."[15] You don't have a say in whether or not you are tempted, but you do have a say in how much and how often. Your goal should be to stay as far away from temptation as you possibly can.

Tammy: A man and a woman in love, all alone, at night, *in bed* — that's just setting you up for failure. Plus, this is the whole point of marriage! It's what you look forward to, and it's more than worth the wait.

Question: What is the biblical view of moving in with someone of the opposite sex before marriage?

Gerry: Genesis 2 is the paradigm. "That is why a man leaves his father and mother and is united to his wife, and they become one flesh. Adam and his wife were both naked, and they felt no shame."[16] God doesn't say, "Leave your parents, move in together, have sex, and cohabitate for a year or two. Then, when you're ready to actually take the plunge, and you've got gobs of money saved up for an expensive wedding and exotic honeymoon, go ahead and get married." No. It's simultaneous. You leave (your family in ancient culture, your roommates today), are "united," and "become one flesh" — all at once. That's why couples who move in together before marriage feel a twinge of shame. Deep down, they know they should get married, not just split rent.

John Mark: Not surprisingly, study after study shows that couples who cohabitate have higher divorce rates.[17] They are actually *less* likely to make marriage work in the long run.

Question: How do you handle dating, engagement, and marriage when one person in the relationship has an extensive sexual history and the other is a virgin? In particular, if the man has slept with many women (one-night stands and long-term relationships) and the woman hasn't, how can they work to overcome the insecurity, hurt, and baggage that accompanies the differences in their pasts?

John Mark: Just the other day I had coffee with a good friend of mine and the girl he is seriously dating. He has a past, and she's a virgin. They were asking the exact same question—"How do we sort through this?"

Like we said before, talk about your past *before* you get serious. The last thing you want on your honeymoon is a string of exposed secrets.

Gerry: The guy needs to confess his sin because it was done against his future spouse. He needs to *feel* the pain he's caused her. The damage he's inflicted. He needs to take it seriously. The girl needs to listen, do the hard work of grieving over her loss, emphasize that his sin is forgiven by God, and then start working to forgive him.

It can be helpful for the guy to break the "soul tie," the life bond, he has with women from his past. He should verbally confess to God and to his girlfriend/fiancée that he is no longer attached to them. He should renounce and reject his past, pray with her, and then they should both stand together for a clean slate. This can be done with the help of a good counselor.

Tammy: Then *after* you've done that, you need to move on. I think of Paul's words to the Philippians—"Forgetting what is behind and straining toward what is ahead, I press on ..."[18] You can't dwell on the past. You gotta unhook your mind and imagination from what happened and fill your thought life with what's to come. This isn't easy. It takes a dogged, unflinching "long obedience in the same direction."[19]

John Mark: Remember that "if anyone is in Christ, the new creation has come."[20] That's not a worn-out cliché. That's the gospel of Jesus at work. If you're a virgin, and you saved yourself, but your spouse-to-be isn't and didn't, this a chance for you to be like Jesus and cover your spouse's sins. Trust me, the time will come when they get to return the favor.

Question: My relationship with God is different from my girlfriend's. She struggles with things I don't, and I struggle with things she doesn't. Is that okay?

Tammy: Oh yeah, healthy even. You're not clones. The whole point of marriage is to offset each other's weak spots in order to serve better. Hopefully, your strengths will rub off on each other in time.

Questions on male and female

Question: Should a woman ever be the one to tell a man she likes him?

John Mark: Sure. This is a cultural question, not a biblical one. Case in point—that's how it *used* to be done in America. It's since changed, but either way is fine. The Scriptures give you all sorts of freedom.

Tammy: If you are the one to instigate, just make sure you tell him in a way that makes him feel respected. I tend to be more old-fashioned by nature. I like the idea of being pursued. But if that's not how you're wired, then just be yourself. Know that strong women can be intimidating to some guys, but by all means, tell him how you feel. This is totally a preference thing, and I don't think it's wrong at all.

Question: How should a single woman interact with single men she may be interested in? How do we let them know we like them without "pursuing"?

John Mark: For starters, I love that you said "men" and not "a single man." Props.

Tammy: I would say smile, make eye contact, and be interested. Ask them questions. When they answer, pay attention and listen. Be friendly. Get away from your circle of girlfriends (which is intimidating for men), and be where he's at. You know how girls travel in packs? *Don't* do that. Make yourself available. "Bump" into him. Do the best you can with what you have, to make yourself a modest but attractive woman. In the words of John Mark's grandma, Mary Sue, "Run just fast enough to get caught."

Question: I'd like to know your thoughts on the Greek words *arsenokoites* and *malakos*, translated "homosexual offenders" and "male prostitutes" in 1 Corinthians 6v9. What do they mean?

Gerry: As you can imagine, over the last ten years there have been multiple attempts to reinterpret these two words found in Paul's writings to mean something other than gay sex. Each one has been shot down by scholarship.

Malakos means "soft" or "effeminate." We think it's speaking of the passive partner in a gay relationship. This could be when a man would dress, smell, and act like a woman to attract a gay man, or it could be in pederasty, when an older male would penetrate a younger boy between the ages of fourteen and seventeen. Both practices were socially acceptable in the ancient Mediterranean world.

Arsenokoites is a compound of two Greek words — *arsen*, which means "male," and *koite*, which means "bed." The idea is a man who goes to bed with another man. Matthew Vines and others argue that this word wasn't used before Paul and that it probably means some kind of abuse or weird sexual depravity. They argue that its meaning changed halfway through the last century, when Bible translators started to connect the word to homosexuality. But that's just not true. Paul coined a very precise word by joining two words from Leviticus 18v22 and 20v13. He used Greek words from the Septuagint, the Greek translation of the Hebrew Bible used by Paul and the New Testament authors. When the two words are put together, it takes us to the Levitical laws about homosexuality. Paul is agreeing and affirming what God already said through Moses.[21]

Question: How can I strongly believe that one-man and one-woman relationships are the only truth when polygamy was a normal and accepted practice in the Bible?

John Mark: This is crucial to get. Some things in the Bible are *descriptive*, while others are *prescriptive*. Polygamy is in the descriptive category. The Bible is just telling what happened. Marriage between one man and one woman is *prescriptive*. Read Genesis 2v24. It's paradigmatic. It's how it's supposed to be.

Gerry: And read the stories about polygamy — every one is a disaster! Sure it was accepted in the ancient Near Eastern culture, but it was never accepted by God. If anything, the Bible is God's commentary on why it's a bad idea. There's not a single polygamous marriage that's painted in a positive light. Every one is a meltdown.

John Mark: Mark Twain was once asked by a Mormon where the Bible explicitly says polygamy is wrong. He fired back, "No man can serve two masters." Well said.

To wrap up ...

Good teaching often sparks as many questions as it does answers. That's why people were always asking Jesus questions ...

"Who can forgive sins but God alone?"[22]

"Rabbi, who sinned, this man or his parents, that he was born blind?"[23]

"Are you the Messiah, the Son of the Blessed One?"[24]

Somehow it's fitting to end with questions. After all, Jesus was a rabbi, or teacher. The Greek word for *disciple* can be translated "learner" or "student." That's what you are, if you follow Jesus. You're a learner. Every day you enroll in the class of life. Listen up — Jesus has some *really* good stuff to say.

Notes

The beginning

1. The divorce rate is a bit unreliable because it's next to impossible to calculate. Most studies say 40 to 50 percent, but that's an average that doesn't reflect the complexity of society. It's kind of like saying the chances of dying from a tornado in the United States are 2 percent. In reality, where I live, the chances are 0 percent, but in Florida, the chances are more like 10 percent (I'm making up these numbers!). In the same way, studies show that couples who are educated, have a middle to high socioeconomic status, live in an urban setting, are religious, don't marry super-young, don't cohabitate before marriage, and are monogamous have *great* odds at a lasting marriage. But couples who have a high school diploma or less, have a low socioeconomic status, marry young, cohabitate before marriage, and live in a rural setting are much more likely to divorce. My point is that the number is *high* by any standards. Here are a few websites to visit if you're interested in learning more. Just about every legit study, journal, or article on divorce rates were based on statistics provided by the Centers for Disease Control, www.cdc.gov/nchs/nvss/marriage_divorce_tables.htm (accessed September 4, 2013). See also the American Psychological Association's *Monitor on Psychology* article titled "Can This Marriage Be Saved?" www.apa.org/monitor/2013/04/marriage.aspx (accessed September 4, 2013). Check out this interesting information about interpreting divorce statistics, www.divorcereform.org/about.html (accessed September 4, 2013).

2. The entire story is found in Matthew 19v1 – 12.

3. Deuteronomy 24v1 – 4.

4. If you're curious why there's all this talk about men divorcing women but nothing about women divorcing men, keep in mind this is in first-century Palestine. It's patriarchal to the core. This is one of the many reasons that Jesus' treatment of women in general, and his teachings on divorce in particular, are good news for women today.

5. This is from Genesis 2. *Such* a riveting story. You should read it. Again.

6. John 8v44; 10v10.

7. So this is from the *next* story, in Genesis 3.

Ahava

1. John 21v7.

2. 1 John 4v10.

3. Hebrews 12v2.

4. I'm pretty sure you know where that one is from — John 3v16, emphasis added.

5. Romans 8v32, emphasis added.

6. Ephesians 5v25, emphasis added.

7. This is found in John 13v1 – 20.

8. John 13v13 – 15.

9. John 13v34, emphasis added.

10. Mark 12v30 – 31.

11. Song of Songs 2v10. We're gonna get to this book in just a bit.

12. It's literally the opening line. Song of Songs 1v1 – 2.

13. Song of Songs 8v6 – 7.

14. *Via dolorosa* is Latin for "way of grief." It's the (supposed) route that Jesus walked to the cross. In the modern-day city of Jerusalem, it winds from the Antonia Fortress through the old city to the Church of the Holy Sepulchre. If you're ever in Jerusalem, you should walk it.

15. Oh, yeah. This is an allusion to my friend Bob Goff's book, *Love Does*. Go read it!

What's the point?

1. That would be from Revelation 21v2. Such a compelling vision.

2. Genesis 2v24, emphasis added.

3. Genesis 2v7 – 8, 15.

4. Genesis 2v18.

5. I'm getting this from the geographical markers we read about in Genesis 2v8 – 15. Obviously, I'm taking a bit of liberty here. We don't know how big it was. The point is, it's huge.

Cuatro

1. Once again, Genesis 2v18.

2. Genesis 1v26, emphasis added.

3. This can be debated a bit. Some people – Jewish rabbis in particular – think God is talking to the angels. The problem is that we're not created in the image of the angels.

4. Deuteronomy 6v4. Technically, the great *Shema* is Deuteronomy 6v4 – 9; 11v31 – 21; and Numbers 15v37 – 41, but people usually just quote the first part.

5. Proverbs 2v17.

6. Genesis 1v26, emphasis added.

7. Genesis 1v28, emphasis added.

8. Once again, I'm getting this idea from Genesis 2v10 – 14.

9. Psalm 118v7, emphasis added.

10. Thinking of Paul's command to wives in Ephesians 5v33.

11. Genesis 2v25.

12. Genesis 5v4.

13. Genesis 1v28. I feel like I'm just quoting *Genesis* over and over and over.

14. Guttmacher Institute, "Facts on Induced Abortion," www.guttmacher .org/pubs/fb_induced_abortion. html#2 (accessed July 24, 2013).

15. National Fatherhood Initiative, "The Father Factor," www.fatherhood .org/media/consequences-of-father -absence-statistics (accessed July 24, 2013).

16. K. J. Dell'Antonia, "For Younger Mothers, Out-of-Wedlock Births Are the New Normal," http://parenting .blogs.nytimes.com/2012/02/19/for -younger-mothers-out-of-wedlock -births-are-the-new-normal/ (accessed July 24, 2013).

Reverse engineering, "the one," and other things – like unicorns

1. Genesis 3v11.

2. John 1v1, 3.

3. Colossians 1v19 – 20, but you should read the entire passage. It's riveting. And it's proof the standard American gospel is *way too small*.

4. 2 Corinthians 5v17.

5. If you want to read more about this idea, pick up my good friend Dave Lomas's book, *The Truest Thing About*

You: Identity, Desire, and Why It All Matters (Colorado Springs: Cook, 2014). It's good stuff.

6. Romans 1v7; Colossians 3v12; 2 Corinthians 11v2; Ephesians 1v4, 11; 1 John 3v1; Romans 8v17.

7. Ephesians 4v1.

8. In the Symposium, the story is actually told by a dude named Aristophanes.

9. Romans 8v3 – 4.

10. At my church, this is called a missional community. Sounds like a cult, but it's actually incredible.

Very good

1. Luke 7v34, by the Pharisees. To clarify, Jesus was neither. Interesting also, the next phrase states he was "a friend of tax collectors and sinners." I think it's odd that we call Jesus a friend of sinners. By that logic he's also a glutton and a drunkard, and the implication is that we should be too. But these were false accusations. Jesus actually said to the disciples, "You are my friends if you do what I command" (John 15v14, emphasis added). The truth is that Jesus is open to all. Sinners were, and still are, comfortable around him. But he's the friend of those who follow him – okay, that was a tangent.

2. 1 Timothy 6v17.

3. Props to my assistant Alex Rettmann for coining the phrase "a theology of enjoyment." Dude, you're a genius.

4. Richard Foster, The Challenge of the Disciplined Life (San Francisco: HarperSanFrancisco, 1989), 163.

5. Genesis 1v27. But it's not the last. In 1 Corinthians 7v1 – 5, Paul commands married couples to have sex on a regular, rhythmic basis.

6. This line comes from my buddy and mentor Mike Erre. Such a great line. Mike's teachings on sexuality are the best I've heard, and they've inspired a lot of this section in the book. If you want to listen for yourself, go to www.evfreefullerton.com/sexloveandgod/ (accessed October 8, 2013).

7. Matthew 14v13 – 21.

8. There's a great section on this in Our Father Abraham: The Jewish Roots of the Christian Faith by Marvin

R. Wilson (Grand Rapids: Eerdmans, 1989), 177.

9. In no way, shape, or form do I mean this as a slam on Catholic priests. Later in the book I'm going to argue that celibacy can be a good thing. I'm just not a fan of the worldview of *mandated* celibacy for priests.

10. That said, marriage as a whole is a metaphor for the Messiah and the church. Paul says that in Ephesians 5. So in that sense, yes, *The Song* is a metaphor or "picture" of God's love for his people and of how we dance with him. But I still see that as the secondary reading of a love poem about a man and a woman.

11. Obviously, some will disagree with me. There's no consensus on the authorship of *Song of Songs*. Some think it was Solomon. The Talmudic tradition points to King Hezekiah, and others argue it's a collection of short poems from a variety of authors and compiled for Solomon. I know a ton of smart, educated people have read it as an allegory, and I don't mean to slam them at all, but I very much disagree. Many people ask how Solomon, a guy with seven hundred wives, could have written this book. That's a hard one. If Solomon is the author (which is up for grabs), it could have been written early in his life. First Kings 1 mentions "Abishag, a Shunammite," a beautiful young virgin who cared for King David as he was dying. Then, in the next chapter, Solomon's ambitious brother, Adonijah, asks to be given Abishag as his wife. Solomon is so enraged by the request that he has Adonijah killed. What's up with that? Jealousy? It could be that Abishag is the historical character behind *The Song* and that this love story takes place early in Solomon's life, before his descent into polygamy and sin. Could be, but there's no way to know if Solomon is the author in the first place. At this point we're well into the realm of theory and opinion. My point is that no ancient Jew would have read this book as an "allegory about Christ and the church." At least, I don't think so.

12. My Bible, the NIV, reads "Friends" above this line. But the heading isn't in the Hebrew, and most scholars think

it's a mistake. Why would friends be in the bedroom? Awkward …

13. Genesis 3v6.

14. Exodus 12v36.

15. Exodus 32v1.

16. David Foster Wallace, This Is Water: Some Thoughts Delivered on a Significant Occasion, about Living a Compassionate Life (New York: Little Brown, 2009), 100 – 101.

17. Romans 1v24 – 25, emphasis added.

18. John 8v32, emphasis added.

Echad

1. Genesis 2v7.

2. The word soul is a can of worms that is way outside the scope of this book. Technically, both animals and humans have a nephesh (the Hebrew word that is sometimes translated "soul"). But I'm using it here in the Western sense of "the immaterial part of a person."

3. Here's a definition of scientism – "the view that the characteristic inductive methods of the natural sciences are the only source of genuine factual knowledge and, in particular, that they alone can yield true knowledge about man and society." That's from Allan Bullock and Stephen Trombley, eds., The New Fontana Dictionary of Modern Thought (New York: HarperCollins, 2000), 775.

4. Genesis 2v24.

5. Genesis 4v1. The NIV reads "made love," which is an accurate interpretation, but the Hebrew word yada literally means "know." The ESV's "now Adam knew Eve" is a tad clearer. Such a beautiful way to put it. And theologically rich.

6. Read 1 Corinthians 6 for the whole story. These are verses 15 – 17.

7. To the south was the Cape of Malea, which was dangerous to sail around. Plus, it was a 202-mile journey. Corinth was called "the bridge of Greece" because it was built on the isthmus bridging the Peloponnese peninsula and the mainland, and connecting the Adriatic and the Aegean seas. The four-and-a-half mile land bridge was short enough that if a ship was small, it could be dragged across the isthmus. Otherwise, it would have to

be unloaded and the cargo carried to another ship before moving on.

8. See Plato, *Phaedo*.

9. 1 Corinthians 6v13.

10. It's actually where we get the word *pornography*.

11. 1 Corinthians 6v13.

12. 1 Corinthians 6v18.

13. 1 Corinthians 6v19 – 20.

Tree of life

1. Yes, that's from the TV series *Portlandia*. Sadly, it's not that far off.

2. Read Judges 13 for the story.

3. Numbers 6v1 – 8. Technically, it says they can't make themselves "unclean on account of them." We're not 100 percent sure what that means, but it probably has something to do with burial rites.

4. Judges 14v6.

5. Exodus 20v3.

6. Leviticus 19v2.

7. This is from the genius Old Testament scholar from Ireland, Christopher Wright. Man, that guy can think. This quote is from *The Mission of God's People* (Grand Rapids: Zondervan, 2010), 125. His thick volume *The Mission of God* (Downers Grove, IL: InterVarsity, 2006) is the seminal work on missiology.

8. Gotta give credit to Matt Chandler for that phrase. I may not be a Calvinist, but man, that guy can preach.

9. C. M. K. Dush, C. L. Cohan, and P. R. Amato, "The Relationship Between Cohabitation and Marital Quality and Stability: Change Across Cohorts?" *Journal of Marriage and Family* 65 (2003): 539 – 49; 1994. See also David G. Blanchflower and Andrew J. Oswald, "Money, Sex and Happiness: An Empirical Study," *Scandinavian Journal of Economics* 106 (2004): 393 – 415; Edward O. Laumann et al., *The Social Organization of Sexuality: Sexual Practices in the United States* (Chicago: University of Chicago Press, 2000); Andrew Cherlin, *Marriage, Divorce, Remarriage*, rev. ed. (Cambridge, MA: Harvard University Press, 1992).

10. 1 Thessalonians 4v3.

11. 1 Thessalonians 4v7, emphasis added.

12. 1 Corinthians 13. This could be an

original by Paul. We don't know. But he doesn't really strike me as the poetry type. I'm guessing 1 Corinthians 13 was well-known in the early church.

13. 1 Timothy 5v1 – 2.

14. Song of Songs 4v9 – 10.

15. Genesis 2v16 – 17, emphasis added.

16. Genesis 3v4 – 5.

The Song

1. Revelation 21v2.

2. Song of Songs 2v8 – 13.

3. That's in 1 Timothy 2v13. That's a hairy passage to interpret, but the gist is that men are called to lead in the church. More on that later.

4. Song of Songs 4v12.

5. Song of Songs 1v4.

6. I love that. There's this stereotype of men as sex-craved brutes and women as not enjoying sex at all. It doesn't have to be that way. Women often enjoy sex far more than men. A ton of it has to do with how you express your sexuality before marriage. For some, brokenness there can rob you of the joy of sex for the rest of your life.

7. Song of Songs 2v6 – 7.

8. 1 Peter 4v8.

9. Song of Songs 1v4.

10. Song of Songs 1v8.

11. Song of Songs 5v9.

12. Song of Songs 3v6 – 7, 10 – 11.

13. Proverbs 24v27.

14. Mathew 7v24 – 27.

Isaac and Rebekah

1. For a good overview of this history, read Beth L. Bailey, *From Front Porch to Back Seat: Courtship in Twentieth-Century America* (Baltimore, MD: Johns Hopkins University Press, 1988).

2. The famous study ("Exploratory Study of Love and Liking and Type of Marriages," *Indian Journal of Applied Psychology* 19 [1982]: 92 – 97) was done by psychologists Usha Gupta and Pushpa Singh of the University of Rajasthan in Jaipur, India. They used the Rubin Love Scale, which is an American rating scale for happiness in marriage, and found that "free choice" marriages start strong but then the love goes down, while arranged marriages

start weak but are equal by five years and twice as strong by ten. Since then, a number of psychologists have done similar studies. Here's one — Pamela C. Regan, Saloni Lakhanpal, and Carlos Anguiano, "Relationship Outcomes in Indian-American Love-Based and Arranged Marriages," *Psychological Reports* 110 (2012): 915 – 24.

3. Genesis 24v12 – 14.

4. Interesting that we also find Jesus at a well with the Samaritan woman.

5. Genesis 24v50.

6. This is from Timothy Keller, *The Meaning of Marriage* (New York: Dutton, 2011), hands down *the best* book I know of on the topic of marriage. It's written to married couples, but still well worth the time for unmarrieds. Seriously, put this book down right now and go out and buy it.

7. INTJ, if you must know.

8. I know this from experience. These are the three other cities in the United States I would love to live in. Of course, if I could live anywhere, it would be London. Hmm …

9. Genesis 24v67.

10. I first read this in Marvin R. Wilson,

Our Father Abraham: Jewish Roots of the Christian Faith (Grand Rapids: Eerdmans, 1989), 202. I've since seen it a bunch of places. I think it's officially reached idiom status.

A form of torture called waiting

1. Pew Research Center, "Pew Research and Social Demographic Trends," www.pewsocialtrends.org/2011/12/14/barely-half-of-u-s-adults-are-married-a-record-low/ (accessed July 24, 2013).

2. Psalm 37v7.

3. James 4v14. I know the imagery of your breath on a cold morning is overused, but that's because it's so good. For those of you who live in California, I'm sorry. You wouldn't understand.

4. That's in Philippians 4v11.

5. The NASB translates it that way.

6. Psalm 37v9 NASB. The NIV reads "those who hope in the LORD."

7. This chapter was inspired by teaching from Louie Giglio — an all-around smart guy. One of the best we have. His series on relationships is called

"Boy Meets Girl" and can be found at www.passioncitychurch.com (accessed September 4, 2013).

X and Y

1. Genesis 1v27. How many times have I quoted this already?
2. *Shaddai* may derive from the Hebrew word *shad*, which means "breast." Some scholars translate *El-Shaddai* as "the breasted One," or "the nourishing One." Read Genesis 49v25; Exodus 6v3; Deuteronomy 32v18; Isaiah 42v14; 49v15; Luke 13v34. That doesn't mean God is asexual. God is spirit.
3. Galatians 3v28. Ironically, some people use this verse to argue that gender roles have been abrogated by the gospel. I think that's a misreading of the text. In context, Paul is not talking about gender roles. He's talking about Jews and Gentiles as one in the church. In the same way that he's not erasing his Jewishness, he's not erasing his maleness.
4. Genesis 2v23.
5. Read Genesis 3.

6. Teresa Blackman, "Study says Portland not a 'manly' city," www.kgw.com/news/Study-says-Portland-not-a-manly-city-96993344.html (accessed September 4, 2013). We fared much better in last year's ranking. See "'America's Manliest Cities' Study," http://americasmanliestcities.com (accessed September 4, 2013).
7. Genesis 2v15.
8. Also in the church in Paul's writings, but that's outside the scope of this book.
9. Genesis 3v20.

War, peace, and why marriage is really about Jesus

1. Genesis 3v16.
2. Ephesians 5v21.
3. Ephesians 5v22 – 24.
4. Ephesians 5v25 – 33.
5. Genesis 3v9.
6. Luke 22v42.
7. Mark 10v5 – 6.

The gift that nobody wants

1. Proverbs 18v22.

2. It's in 1 Corinthians 7. Most of the chapter is written to "the unmarried."

3. A number of scholars think *2 Corinthians* is actually a composite of two or three letters from Paul that were written after *1 Corinthians*. It's hard to know with that letter. I lean toward unity in *2 Corinthians*, but either way, Paul was writing to this church a lot!

4. 1 Corinthians 7v7, emphasis added. I added the word *single* to give context. And FYI, all the Scriptures I'm about to quote are from the rest of this chapter.

5. This is because before following Jesus, Paul was a part of the Sanhedrin, a group of Jewish religious leaders. We have a few ancient writings that say you had to be married to be in the group. Plus, in 1 Corinthians 7 Paul specifically addresses widows and the divorced, not just singles in general. This could come out of his own life experience.

6. 1 Corinthians 7:29–31, emphasis added.

7. If this sounds new to you, please, *please*, PLEASE go read N. T. Wright's *Surprised by Hope* (New York: HarperCollins, 2008). It wrecked my life years ago, in the best way. I pray it does the same for you.

8. His name is Jon Viducich, and he has now returned home after three years in Africa and just got engaged to an amazing girl named Lindsey Goff. Her dad wrote a book called *Love Does* a while back. It's a pretty cool family.

9. 1 Corinthians 7v33–35.

10. 1 Corinthians 7v8–9, 36.

11. 1 Corinthians 7v26–28.

12. 1 Corinthians 7v39.

13. Proverbs 4v23.

14. 2 Corinthians 6v14–15. The context here is way broader than marriage, but marriage is the ultimate "yoke."

15. 2 Corinthians 6v17–18.

16. 1 Corinthians 7v35.

Gay

1. This is all from Paul's letter to the Romans, chapter 1.

2. Romans 1v26–27.

3. All of these names have been changed for confidentiality, but they are real people in my life.

4. That would be the one and only Rick McKinley. Legend.

5. Romans 3v22–23.

6. 1 John 5v16. Crazy line. Important to get.

7. Romans 1v28–31.

8. Obvious exceptions would be guys like Francis Chan and David Platt. These guys are legit. Thank God there is a growing movement away from materialism in the American church. I find its message deeply convicting, which means it's spot-on.

9. If you wanna see it, go to NBC News.com, "Rick Warren: Pastor in the Political Spotlight," www.nbcnews.com/id/28298093/ns/dateline_nbc-newsmakers/t/rick-warren-pastor-political-spotlight/ (accessed August 5, 2013).

10. We adopted her from Uganda through America World Adoption. Incredible experience.

11. I was first exposed to this way of thinking by Jenell Williams Paris in *The End of Sexual Identity: Why Sex Is Too Important to Define Who We Are* (Downers Grove, IL: InterVarsity, 2011). This is one of the best books I've read on the subject. Her critique of both sides is much needed.

12. Also not her real name.

13. For those of you who know my dad, this is hyperbole. He did play in a band in the 1960s, but as far as I know, he was never at Woodstock. If he was, I don't want to know.

14. Most of this section was inspired by Dale Kuehne's *Sex and the iWorld: Rethinking Relationship beyond an Age of Individualism* (Grand Rapids: Baker, 2009).

15. Hebrews 4v15.

16. If you want to read up on sexual ethos in the first-century Mediterranean world, two of the best historians out there are Rodney Stark and Wayne Meeks. Both of these guys have great stuff and are well respected in the academic world. Start with *The Moral World of the First Christians* by Meeks (Louisville, KY: Westminster John Knox, 1986), and go from there.

17. For the last few decades in scholarship, it was assumed there was no ancient equivalent to gay marriage – lifelong, monogamous relationships between gay couples. But recent find-

ings are calling that into question. See the resources in the next endnote.

18. Suetonius, *The Twelve Caesars*, Nero, XXVIII; Cassius Dio, *Roman History*, LXII, 13.

19. There's a bunch of stuff out there you can read. For exegetical arguments, you can start with Thomas E. Schmidt, *Straight and Narrow: Compassion and Clarity in the Homosexuality Debate* (Downers Grove, IL: InterVarsity, 1995), and with Daniel A. Helminiak, *What the Bible* Really *Says about Homosexuality* (Tajique, NM: Alamo Square, 2000).

20. This is Jason Thompson, who leads a local ministry (Portland Fellowship) to gays and lesbians in the church. God is using his story to bring healing to a lot of people in our church and our city; visit www.portlandfellowship.com (accessed August 5, 2013).

21. 1 Corinthians 6v9 – 11.

22. If that describes you, read Wesley Hill's *Washed and Waiting: Reflections on Christian Faithfulness and Homosexuality* (Grand Rapids: Zondervan, 2010), and talk to somebody as soon as you can. Don't hold it inside.

23. This is in Mark 8v34 – 36, as well as in Matthew 16 and Luke 9. It was, and is, the invitation of Jesus.

24. Romans 8v23. Love this passage. Longing for resurrection at a cosmic level.

25. I'm alluding to Matthew 25v21.

Epilogue

1. This story is found in Genesis 25v19 – 34.

2. This one is found in Genesis 29, a few chapters later. Give it a read.

3. Genesis 29v10 – 11.

4. Genesis 29v16 – 18.

5. It's interesting that the narrator of *Genesis* seems to cast the love story of Jacob and Rachel in a negative light. It could be a critique of marriages based on romantic love, or it could just be a critique of Jacob and his life in general. The latter is probably more likely. Still, I think it's interesting that there are only a handful of examples of romantic love (in the way we think about it). One is *Song of Songs*, which is overwhelmingly positive, but the others are Jacob and Rachel, and Samson

and, interestingly, two different women. Samson was "in love" twice, both times with women he should have stayed away from. That's worth thinking about …

6. The story is found in Mark 12v18–27.

7. Mark 12v20–23.

8. Just to clarify, this story is hypothetical. At least, I hope it is!

9. Mark 12v24–26, emphasis added.

10. Matthew 19v28. One of my favorite lines in the Bible for speaking about the future. This is not "in heaven"; this is *after* heaven, at the resurrection, when we live on the earth made new.

11. And that's just in Revelation 22v1–5.

12. Revelation 5v9.

13. Revelation 21v3.

14. That would be Paul in 1 Timothy 6v19.

15. Revelation 21v4. Seriously, if you're ever depressed, you should read the last two chapters of the Bible every day.

16. Isaiah 51v11.

17. This language comes from Luke 12v46.

18. From one of the last paragraphs in the Bible, in Revelation 22v17.

Q and A

1. From Dallas Willard, *The Divine Conspiracy: Rediscovering Our Hidden Life in God* (San Francisco: HarperSanFrancisco, 1997), 165. This guy was a genius. One of my top three favorite books of all time.

2. Matthew 5v27–30 is the section on lust and adultery of the heart, but you need to read the whole sermon to get the context.

3. Philippians 4v8.

4. This language is from Exodus 34v6–7, the most quoted verses in the Bible by the Bible. God's words in these verses are quoted or paraphrased in many other Scriptures (e.g., Numbers 14v18; Nehemiah 9v17; Psalms 86v15; 103v8; 145v8; Joel 2v13; Jonah 4v2). I've done a series based on these verses called "God Has a Name." If you want to learn more about what God is like, feel free to listen at www.ajesuschurch.org/

teaching-past (accessed August 5, 2013).

5. Leviticus 16v20 – 22.

6. Mark 10v11 – 12.

7. Mark 14v36.

8. Song of Songs 2v7; 3v5; 8v4.

9. Matthew 5v29 – 30.

10. The line right before that – Matthew 5v28. Context is everything!

11. For the sin lists, read Mark 7v20 – 23; Romans 1v28 – 32; 1 Corinthians 6v9 – 11.

12. We read Ed Wheat, MD, and Gaye Wheat's *Intended for Pleasure: Sex Technique and Sexual Fulfillment in Christian Marriage* (Grand Rapids: Revell, 2010). Gerry likes Kevin Leman's *Sheet Music: Uncovering the Secrets of Sexual Intimacy in Marriage* (Wheaton, IL: Tyndale House, 2003).

13. Mark 10v45.

14. 1 Corinthians 13v7 in the NASB.

15. James 1v14 – 15, emphasis added.

16. Genesis 2v24 – 25.

17. Alfred DeMaris and K. Vaninadha Rao, "Premarital Cohabitation and Subsequent Marital Stability in the United States: A Reassessment," *Journal of Marriage and the Family* 54 (1992): 178 – 90; see also Zheng Wu, *Cohabitation: An Alternative Form of Family Living* (New York: Oxford University Press, 2000), 149.

18. Philippians 3v13 – 14. Such a good word, no matter where you're coming from.

19. These words come originally from Nietzsche's *Beyond Good and Evil* and are found in the title of one of Eugene Peterson's many books (*A Long Obedience in the Same Direction* [Downers Grove, IL: InterVarsity, 1980]).

20. 2 Corinthians 5v17.

21. For more info, read Robert Gagnon, *The Bible and Homosexual Practice: Texts and Hermeneutics* (Nashville: Abingdon, 2001).

22. Mark 2v7.

23. John 9v2.

24. Mark 14v61.

Thanks

My wife, Tammy, for picking up the pen. Your love has been unswerving through it all. Twelve down, fifty to go. I'll say it again and again and again — *I love you*.

Jude, Moses, and Sunday, for filling up my heart with more joy than I ever thought possible.

My family, for Christmas mornings, date nights, and #campcomer.

Bill and Laurie Keyes, for saving our marriage, one DISC test at a time.

My MC family — the Normans, Fullers, Bradys, and Petersons — you are one of the best things that's ever happened to us. We *love* doing life with you. Here's to kale chips, Linsey's cooking, block parties, and living out the gospel together.

Matt Norman, for being a better friend to me than anybody ever has. You're more like Jesus than any guy I know. 6:45 tomorrow morning?

Ian Nelson, for reading first drafts, saving me on my Hebrew home-work, and being the nicest genius on the planet.

Dr. Gerry Breshears, for putting up with me in cohort! Seriously, you have been my mentor, my pastor, and my friend. I'm forever in your debt.

Mike Erre, for showing me the ropes. Here's to Powell's, Gravy, and Disneyland.

Todd Proctor, for your friendship. (And that house on Balboa Island!)

Bridgetown: A Jesus Church, and our family of churches in Portland, for loving and following Jesus — the real one, not the made up one(s). You're incredible. And you're just crazy enough to believe that God can change this city. Let's never stop praying, *In Portland as it is in heaven ...*

The leadership of AJC — you guys are my coworkers and my friends. I can't imagine a better team to serve alongside. Spirit, come ...

The crew at Zondervan — Carolyn McCready, Tracy Danz, David, Dirk, John, Tom, and the rest — for taking a chance on me. You've been fantastic. All of you. Tracy, I'm still loving that Eames book.

And above all ...

Jesus, for coming as Love-incarnate.

John Mark Comer is the pastor for teaching and vision at Bridgetown: A Jesus Church, which is part of a family of churches in Portland, Oregon. It's a city of coffee, food, culture, indie bands, and depressed people—he fits right in.

Prior to planting Bridgetown in 2003, John Mark was the college pastor at a megachurch in Southern Oregon and played in a band. He is the author of *My Name Is Hope: Anxiety, Depression, and Life after Melancholy* and is wrapping up a master's degree in biblical and theological studies at Western Seminary.

John Mark lives in Portland with his wife, Tammy, and their three children, Jude, Moses, and Sunday.

For more of John Mark's teachings on the Scriptures, Jesus, and life, go to ajesuschurch.org and sign up for the podcast or visit www.johnmarkcomer.com.

Loveology study guide with DVD

Well, you've read the book. Good work. But that's just the beginning, right? There's always more to learn, more to know, more to become.

I and the fine folks at Zondervan have put together a *Loveology* video study for you to work through with your friends, family, small group, or missional community. It's basically a map for a conversation around marriage, sex, and relationships.

There are five sessions for you and your friends to talk through — love, marriage, sex, romance, and singleness.

Plus, there's extra stuff for you to think about during the week.

If that sounds interesting, have at it ...

Available in stores and online.

ZONDERVAN
.com